HER STORY II WOMEN FROM CANADA'S PAST

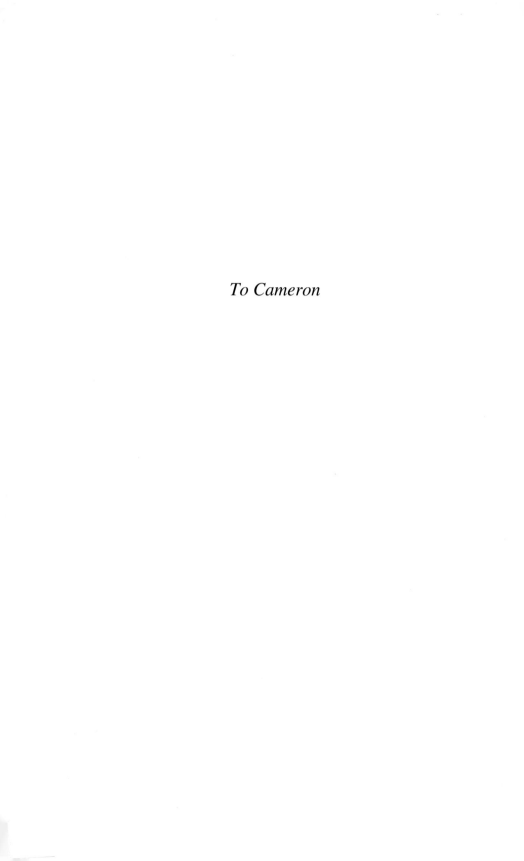

To Cameron

HER STORY II

WOMEN FROM CANADA'S PAST

Susan E Merritt

Vanwell Publishing Limited
St. Catharines, Ontario

Canadian Cataloguing in Publication Data

Merritt, Susan E.
    Her story II: women from Canada's past

Includes bibliographical references and index.
ISBN 1-55125-022-5

1.   Women - Canada - History - Juvenile literature.
2.   Indian women - Canada - Biography - Juvenile
literature. 3. Women, Black - Canada - Biography -
Juvenile literature. 4. Women immigrants -
Canada - Biography - Juvenile literature.
5. Europeans - Canada - Biography - Juvenile
literature. I. Title.

FC26.W6M42 1995   j305.4'092'271   C95-931888-7
F1005.M42 1995

Design Linda L. Moroz
Maps Angela A. Irvine

Vanwell Publishing Limited
1 Northrup Crescent
P.O. Box 2131
St. Catharines, Ontario   L2M 6P5

First Edition Printed 1995
Printed in Canada

Cover: Detail of A Meeting of the School Trustees
Copyright©National Gallery of Canada

*Special Thanks to the staff of the National Library of Canada and of the
Fort Erie Public Library.*

CONTENTS

INTRODUCTION

Whenever you read a history book ask yourself,"Where are the women?" Chances are, they will not have been included. Women may form the majority of the population, but they are often invisible in history books. Even when they are mentioned, the obstacles women faced as a group are rarely discussed, and their lives and achievements are rarely celebrated. Yet whether you are male or female, *half* of your ancestors were female. How did your female ancestors live? What did they do? How did they contribute to the world around them? The answers may surprise you.

I wrote my first book, *Her Story: Women from Canada's Past,* as a celebration of the courage, strength and determination of women. I soon discovered there were too many interesting women to fit into one volume. As a result, I have written *Her Story II: Women From Canada's Past*, which contains another sixteen biographies of women from Canadian history. Once again, however, size restrictions meant I could not include all the interesting women I discovered during my research.

Like *Her Story*, *Her Story II* contains biographies of women born before or around 1900, who are of First Nations, black, or European ancestry. Every province, as well as the Northwest Territories, is connected with at least one woman in *Her Story II*. Each chapter can stand completely on its own and the book may be read in any order.

The life stories of the women in this book include joys and sorrows, hardships and achievements. Some of the women are authors, reformers, midwives, photographers, or pioneers. Some refused to accept the narrow roles that society handed women and, in spite of many obstacles, became artists, doctors, politicians or scientists. This book is a celebration of the life and times of these fascinating women.

Where are the women in Canadian history? *Her Story II* provides some of the answers.

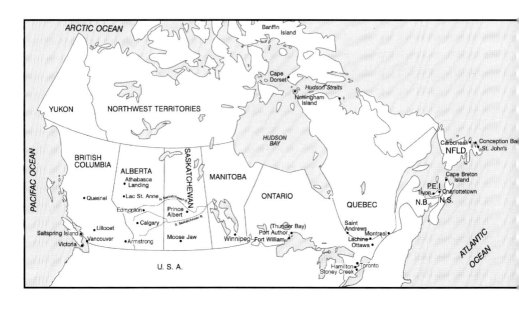

CHAPTER 1

MOHAWK BY CHOICE

EUNICE WILLIAMS
—— (1696 - 1785) ——

When white persons of either sex are taken prisoners young by the Indians, in a short time they become disgusted with our manner of life and ... there is no reclaiming them.

—Benjamin Franklin

"Do you pray to God every day, child?" Reverend John Williams asked severely. He was shocked to see his daughter Eunice, now brown from the sun, wearing Native clothing. Yet he had to admit she looked healthy and happy. Too happy.

Eunice stood beside the black-haired woman she loved and called mother, and calmly examined Reverend Williams. He wanted her to go with him, this long-ago father who did not smile. But he looked pale and harsh and Eunice wanted to forget the long ago, for now she was happy.

Eunice looked Reverend Williams in the eye. "It is time for you to go away," she said firmly. "I am Mohawk now."

PURITAN BY BIRTH

Eunice Williams was born in Deerfield, Massachusetts, on 17 September 1696. Her parents were John Williams, a Puritan minister, and Eunice Mather Williams.

The Puritans were a group of English Protestants who believed that the Church of England did not practise Christianity as simply as it should be practised. They argued that the Christian faith should return to its "ancient purity." Many Puritans wanted to remain in the Church of England and reform it from within, but one group wanted to separate. The Church of England called these people "Separatists"; they called themselves the "Pilgrims," and their leaders are known as the "Pilgrim Fathers." After a great deal of persecution and suffering for their religious beliefs, the Pilgrims set sail on a ship named the Mayflower and arrived on Cape Cod, in what is now the American state of Massachusetts, in November of 1620. There they set up the Plymouth Colony.

Before long, other English Puritans began emigrating to the New World in search of religious freedom. In 1630 alone, more than a thousand

1.1 Young Eunice Williams may have played with a corn husk doll similar to the one shown here.

1.2 The First Women: Chippewa or Ojibwa

arrived in the Massachusetts Bay area to start a new life. These new Puritans eventually absorbed the little Plymouth Colony.

THE PURITANS AND THE FIRST NATIONS

Life for Eunice and her family would not have been easy. Although land was plentiful and rich, survival was a constant struggle. Floods or droughts could mean starvation, and disease often struck suddenly, killing strong and weak alike.

For the New England Puritans, enemy attack was another ever-present fear. Puritans had often clashed with the local First Nations, who resented the invasion of their lands. In the mid-1600s they had fought the Wampanoag, the Abenaki, the Massachusetts and the Mohegans. In some cases, the Puritans had surprised and massacred men, women and children of the Pequot and the Narragansett nations. In addition to fighting a number of local First Nations, the Puritans, as residents of British colonies, were also swept into the wars of Europe.

WAR IN THE OLD WORLD, WAR IN THE NEW WORLD

France and England were long-time enemies. Over several centuries, they fought many wars, including one which began in Europe in 1702. This war, known as "Queen Anne's War" or "The

War of Spanish Succession," could not be ignored by the settlers in the British and French colonies of North America.

War was profitable for some colonists. It gave fur traders an excuse to enlarge their territory. As well, it gave Boston ship owners the chance to engage in state-approved piracy: they could send their vessels out as "privateers" and turn a tidy profit by capturing enemy ships and robbing enemy towns.

However, for the ordinary men, women and children of New France, New England and the First Nations, European wars often meant hardship and disaster.

KIDNAPPED!

Kidnapping enemy inhabitants and holding them for ransom, a practice that both Government and Church encouraged, also made war a profitable event. In February or early March of 1704, a force of 340 French, Abenaki and Kahnawake Mohawk men attacked the snow-covered New England town of Deerfield. They killed 42 of the inhabitants, burned 17 houses and took 112 prisoners. Among the prisoners were Eunice Williams, who was only seven at the time, her parents and four other children of the family.

The forced march north to New France must have been terrifying for the captives. The French and First Nations

1.3 The First Women: Sarcee

1.4 The First Women: unidentified nation

kidnappers were fit and strong, and used to travelling rapidly through the woods in all kinds of weather. They were also worried about being captured themselves as long as they remained in enemy territory. As a result, the raiding party travelled north at exhausting speeds. The captives, shocked and grieving, had been taken from their homes without food supplies or suitable clothing for the knee deep snow. The New Englanders were not used to the rapid travel or the food and flimsy shelter their captors shared with them. Eunice's mother and 17 other captives who were unable to keep up were killed along the way. This was not as cruel an act as it may seem. The survival of the other captives as well as that of the kidnappers was at stake. Those who could not keep up had to be left behind, and a quick death was preferable to a lingering one from exposure and starvation, or to becoming prey for wild animals. Reverend Williams later wrote that Eunice "was carried all the journey and looked after with a great deal of tenderness," as was her four-year-old brother.

Once they reached the Montreal area, Eunice and her family were separated and sent to live with different French and First Nation families. They were held by these families until their freedom was purchased.

THE KIDNAPPING BUSINESS

Taking captives was often the main function of First Nation war parties; warriors sometimes took along extra moccasins for the prisoners they hoped to seize. It is estimated that during the wars between New England and New France, over 1600 people were kidnapped from New England. While some died in captivity, many were ransomed back to the English. Other captives lived the rest of their lives in New France. Still others, with last names such as Gill, McGregor, Rice, Tarbell, Williams, Hill, Stacey and Jacobs were adopted by First Nation communities.

Among the First Nations, taking captives was a long established practice did more than just terrify and weaken the enemy. Adopting captives to take the place of dead relatives was one way that a First Nation could keep its own population from dropping to dangerously low levels.

Eunice was taken by her Mohawk captors to Kahnawake (also written Caughnawaga) on the south shore of the St. Lawrence River across from Montreal.

THE MOHAWKS OF KAHNAWAKE

The Mohawks, a leading nation of the powerful Iroquois or Six Nations, were traditionally enemies of the French. There is, however, a reason why the Mohawks of Kahnawake sided with the French in war. When Jacques Cartier sailed up the St. Lawrence River in 1535, he had visited the important town of Hochelaga that was home to several thousand people of the First Nations. Some believe Cartier's brief visit introduced new and deadly European diseases that ravaged the town's inhabitants. By the time Samuel de Champlain arrived in 1603, the once-thriving town of Hochelaga had vanished, and French colonists built Montreal in its place.

By the 1640s there was a Mohawk town across the river from Montreal. Known as Kahnawake, meaning "By the rapids," it was near the Roman Catholic mission of Sault-Saint-Louis. Many of the Mohawks living in Kahnawake had been converted by the Jesuits to Christianity. As well, Roman Catholic converts of other Iroquois nations sometimes moved to Kahnawake to avoid the taunts and jeers of non-Christians. Living where they did, under the influence of the French priests, the Mohawks of Kahnawake, also known as the Christian Mohawks or the Mission Iroquois, often sided with the French in war.

ADOPTION

Many First Nations had a formal adoption ceremony for the captives who had been chosen to join their nation. The ceremony of washing captives and dressing them in First Nations clothing was seen as washing the "white blood from their veins." From

1.5 The First Women: Cree

1.6 The First Women: Sioux

that point the captives became full members of the nation.

The Iroquois were divided into clans headed by powerful Clan Mothers. Adoptees belonged to the clan of their adoptive family. Once a formal adoption took place, the adoptee's children were also recognized as full members of the nation. This was an important matter for the children of female adoptees, as the Iroquois traced their ancestry and their clan membership through their mothers, not their fathers.

Eunice Williams was adopted by the Kahnawake Mohawk family that had captured her. She was given the name Gannenstenhawi, which means "She brings in the corn."

Eunice's father and her brothers and sisters were eventually freed. John Williams tried to have Eunice ransomed but he was told by the Jesuit priest at Kahnawake that the Mohawks "would as soon part with their hearts as with the child." He even spoke with young Eunice, but she refused to leave her adoptive family. In 1706, John Williams returned to New England without her but he continued to hope that Eunice would one day return.

PURITAN TALES

John Williams returned to Deerfield as a minister and in 1707 published a book about the attack on Deerfield and his time in Canada. His book, The redeemed captive, returning to Zion, became the best-known example of a type of literature that was widely read in the 1700s and early 1800s: the personal story of captivity among the First Nations.

Early captivity accounts were heavily influenced by the Puritan view of life, and helped to unfairly establish stereotypes of the First Nations as bloodthirsty and cruel. Most of these tales portrayed the First Nations as terrifying symbols of evil rather than as human beings who were capable of both good and bad.

The Puritans saw themselves as waging a Holy War in the "wilderness" of the New World. They viewed the First Nations as the agents of Satan and their raids as divine punishment upon Puritan communities that had somehow strayed from the path of righteousness. Puritans saw captivity among the First Nations as God's way of testing their will power as Christians.

Captives who eventually returned to their homes were used by Puritan ministers as examples of Christians who were "redeemed" by a merciful and powerful God. It must have been difficult, therefore, for John Williams to discover that his daughter Eunice, of her own free will, would not leave her Mohawk family. All attempts to ransom Eunice had failed and spies had reported that she was in good health, "but seemed unwilling to returne, and the Indian not very willing to part with her." The Puritans portrayed the First Nations as cruel. But if Eunice's captors were cruel, why would she, and other New England captives, freely remain with them?

BRUTAL TIMES

Iroquois men were raised to be hunters and fighters. They took pride in enduring pain, hunger and exhaustion without complaint. At times some tortured their captives. A captive Iroquois warrior, however, viewed his own torture as a chance to display his courage. This attitude was not part of European culture, and the prospect of torture terrified all newly captured Europeans.

European captives, however, were often well treated by raiding party members. The ransom value of the prisoners in New France and the chance of later adoption kept many captives from harm. Puritan tales portrayed First Nations warriors as raping captive women, but this was not the case. A warrior would not rape a captive woman for she might be adopted by his own clan and sex between clan members was viewed as incest and strictly forbidden. As well, warriors who were part of raiding parties refused to engage in sex.

Although Europeans feared torture, they were certainly used to the spectacle of torture in those brutal times. In New France, crowds watched "unbelievers" and "witches" burned at the stake. A serious criminal offender could be tied to a wheel and clubbed to death, while minor offenders were flogged or branded in public.

In New England the Puritans, who had come to the New World seeking religious freedom, would not grant that same freedom to others. Puritans persecuted other religious groups such as the Quakers, who were pacifists and believed in religious tolerance. Early Quakers who fell into Puritan hands were sometimes beaten or flayed with tarred ropes; some were branded on the face, blinded or had their ears sliced off; others were hanged.

Puritans also believed that any happening that was out of the ordinary was concrete proof of unseen forces at work. Good events, such as a bountiful harvest, were seen as God's blessing on His people. Major catastrophes were His punishment. Lesser bad events, such as an overturned hay wagon or the sudden death of a cow, were believed to be caused by witches who were the human agents of Satan. Those accused of witchcraft were often publicly tortured and executed by the Puritans. The most famous witchcraft executions in the New World took place at Salem, Massachusetts, only four years before the birth of Eunice Williams. At that time, nineteen people accused of witchcraft were hanged or crushed to death.

In North America, no one group had a monopoly on cruelty and torture.

"WHITE INDIANS"

By 1713, Eunice had married a Mohawk named Arosen. She had adopted the Mohawk language and way of life, and refused to go to Deerfield to see her father. John Williams, however, travelled to New France in 1714 and met with his daughter for the last time. Eunice would not leave her chosen people.

Other captives willingly became members of a First Nation. A Shawnee and French raiding party captured fifteen-year-old Mary Jemison in 1758. She was adopted by two Seneca sisters, married a Seneca leader and lived her life as an Iroquois. Since the Iroquois inherited through their mother's line rather than their father's, Mary's descendants, like those of Eunice Williams, used and passed on the last name of their *female* European ancestor.

Cynthia Ann Parker was captured and adopted as a child by the Comanche. Known by Texas settlers as "The White Comanche" she married a chief and refused to be ransomed. While hunting buffalo with other Comanche women, she was captured by settlers. Although her brother built her a cabin next to his own, she tried to escape back to the Comanche several times before she died.

Apaches captured Olive Oatman as a child and sold her to the Mohave people. Years later, European settlers captured her and took her away from the Mohaves. One of the settlers wrote, "At every opportunity [she tried] to flee back to her Indian husband and children ... For four years she lived with us but she was a grieving, unsatisfied woman who somehow shook one's belief in civilization."

MOHAWK TO THE END

In 1740, 1741 and 1761, Eunice and various members of her First Nations family visited Longmeadow, Massachusetts, where her brother Stephen was a minister. She always refused, however, to permanently leave her Kahnawake home. Today her Iroquois descendants still live in Kahnawake and St. Regis. Eunice Williams, Puritan by birth and Mohawk by choice, died in Kahnawake at the age of eighty-nine.

Further suggested reading on the Mohawk nation:

Bonvillan, Nancy. *The Mohawk*. New York: Chelsea House Publications, 1992.

CHAPTER 2

MIDWIFE AND HEALER

MARIE-HENRIETTE LEJEUNE ROSS

—————— (1762 - 1860) ——————

There is a tender regard one woman bears to another, and a natural sympathy in those that have gone thro' the Pangs of Childbearing; which, doubtless, occasion a compassion for those that labour under these circumstances, which no man can be a judge of.
— **Sarah Stone,** *A Complete Practice of Midwifery* **(London, 1737)**

Marie-Henriette woke with a jolt to the sound of someone pounding on her door. "Granny Ross! Granny Ross! Mama's time has come upon her early. Please come!" The child's cry ended with a sob of relief as Marie-Henriette pulled open the cabin door.

A little girl, her face tear-stained and her eyes wide with terror, stood outside in the doorway, panting from her long run. "Why it's la petite Louise! Little one, you have travelled far by night on your mother's behalf. Of course I will come."

This early labour was a bad sign, Marie-Henriette thought, as she hurriedly dressed for the journey. It was plain that Louise's mother was worn out from too many births and too much work. Would the dawn bring a new life into the community? Or would the exhausted woman die in childbirth and the baby with her? The midwife saw a never-ending cycle of birth and death, thought Marie-Henriette grimly as she pulled on her cloak.

"Come Louise." She held out her hand to the child. "You have been very brave tonight. And now, ma petite, you must be brave some more. You and I, we must show great courage." Marie-Henriette held up a pine torch to light the path and the two slipped away into the darkness.

ACADIA

For over a century the land of Acadia (now Nova Scotia and New Brunswick) was continually fought over by the French and British. The Acadians, the French settlers in this Atlantic maritime region, generally tried to remain neutral in any conflict. They succeeded reasonably well until the mid-1750s when the two powers began to wage the last of their wars in North America. By then, the British had controlled Acadia for more than forty years. Through all that time, the Acadians had peacefully gone about their business of tending their farms and raising their families. However, the British mistrusted them and demanded that they take an oath of allegiance to the British Crown.

The oath required them to fight against the French in wartime, and the Acadians, who felt they might end up in French hands again, refused to take it. In response, the British deported the Acadians so that they could not help the enemy. By mid-1758, the Acadian people had been scattered far and wide, some to Europe, most to parts of Britain's other North American colonies.

Among the deportees were Joseph Lejeune and his wife, Martine Le Roi Lejeune. They were taken to France where their daughter, Marie-Henriette, was born in 1762. The Acadians were used to a rich and bountiful land, and those in France found it difficult to farm that country's often overused soil. As well, the rigid laws did not allow men to take up more than one occupation. Acadian men, used to combining farming with fishing or fishing with carpentry, were taken to court in France if they tried to do the same there. As a result, many Acadians were unhappy in France and waited for a chance to return to North America.

While Marie-Henriette was still a baby, her family and other Acadians recrossed the Atlantic and settled on the tiny French islands of Saint-Pierre and Miquelon, off the south coast of Newfoundland. The French government, however, soon ordered them to leave the overcrowded islands. The Lejeune family moved back to Cape Breton Island, even though settlement there was illegal.

Eleven years later, conditions had improved on Miquelon and Marie-Henriette and her family returned to live on the tiny French island. Their ordeals were not over, however.

During the American Revolution, France supported the rebels and British forces attacked Saint-Pierre and Miquelon. They set the buildings on fire and deported all of the inhabitants, including sixteen-year-old Marie-Henriette, to France. The displaced Acadians were no happier there than they had been earlier. In 1783, at the end of the revolution, the Lejeune family returned to Miquelon. There, Marie-Henriette's first husband drowned.

In 1785, Marie-Henriette and her family resettled in Cape Breton. Marie-Henriette remarried, but her second husband died within a few years. In 1793, she married James Ross, who had fought on the British side in the American Revolution.

Marie-Henriette spent the rest of her life on Cape Breton Island, where she became known as "Granny Ross," and her skills as a midwife and healer became legendary.

WOMEN AS HEALERS

In early times, women were often the community healers. The art of healing required skill, gentleness and wisdom, which were viewed as natural characteristics of motherhood. Women healers knew how to dress burns, poultice wounds, treat toothaches and frostbite, induce vomiting, reduce swelling, administer an enema and tend to diseases such as measles and whooping cough.

In early times women were also community pharmacists. They looked at the world around them and believed that there was a plant to cure each ailment. They experimented and observed the healing properties of various plants and trained their female relatives in the art of using them. Some women were so knowledgeable about the healing properties of many roots and herbs that they became celebrated healers, known as "wise women."

As the type and amount of chemicals that the healing plants contained could vary according to the season, it was important to collect the plants at the proper time. These were then used to manufacture medicine in the form of salves, syrups, pills, teas, ointments, oil emulsions and poultices. Some of the remedies were pure superstition, but some of the wise women's medicines, such as ergot, digitalis and belladonna, are still in use today.

European settlers often learned about the healing properties of North American plants from native healers. In Nova Scotia, Marie-Henriette and other healers used peppermint or spearmint for colds, balsam fir or burdock roots for boils, cucumber juice for sunburn and tansy for blood poisoning. Other plants, including marigold, yarrow, celandine, life-of-man, camomile, wormwood, balm, heal-all, dandelion and pennyroyal, had their uses too.

Women healers also brought their skills to help other women in the risky, sometimes deadly, business of childbirth.

MIDWIVES

For thousands of years most human beings were delivered by midwives, as the trained women who help other women give birth are called. All matters pertaining to fertility and childbirth were seen as a natural part of a woman's world. Midwives were often older women who had given birth themselves, but whose children were now grown.

During Marie-Henriette's time, birth control was almost unknown, and a married woman was pregnant for most of her childbearing years. Death was the invisible partner in many marriage beds, for giving birth was risky for both mother and child. Like Marie-Henriette, many female healers were also midwives and they used medicinal roots and herbs in childbirth as well.

Through the ages, nothing was more important to the life of the average woman than the skills of her midwife. The mother of Socrates, the ancient Greek philosopher, was a highly respected midwife. However, the status of women healers and midwives also rose and fell with the status of women within their culture.

2.1 Giving birth was a risky, sometimes deadly procedure for mother and child. For generations, women's lives depended on the skills of the midwife.

2.2 The major role of a married woman was to bear children. Married women were pregnant for much of their adult life and there were no guarantees. Each pregnancy could result in birth and life, or birth and death.

THE FRENZY

Women in general, and midwives in particular, were persecuted in Europe during the Middles Ages after *Malleus Maleficarum (The Hammer of Witches)* was published in 1484. The authors, two German Dominican monks, raged against all women as evil, and in particular wrote that midwives "surpass all others in wickedness." Offering medicine to ease the pain of childbirth was a crime; women were *supposed* to suffer in childbirth because the woman Eve had sinned in the Garden of Eden. Both the Protestant and Catholic Church used the *Malleus* as a manual for witch hunts.

With the approval of both Church and Government, so-called "confessions" were extracted from those accused of witchcraft under brutal torture that no one could withstand. The victims were then executed, often burned alive at the stake. Hundreds of thousands of people, some estimate millions, died in the witch-hunting frenzy that swept through Germany, Italy, France and England for several centuries. Of those executed during this time, 85 percent were women and children.

MARIE-HENRIETTE AND THE "RED DEATH"

The witch-hunting frenzy was over by the time of Marie-Henriette's birth. In North America in the early 1800s, there were few medical schools; anyone who wished to heal could do so. In the Maritime region, talented women such as Marie-Henriette were given the title "Aunt'"or "Granny" as a sign of respect.

Marie-Henriette first established her reputation as a healer when a smallpox epidemic swept through the Bras d'Or area where she lived. Smallpox was a highly contagious disease that began with the influenza-like symptoms of chills, fever, backache and headache. Within another three to five days, however, the patient's skin turned hot and red, and pus-filled blisters, known as *pox*, began to emerge. Eventually the blisters crusted over with scabs, and when the scabs fell off, the skin was often deeply scarred and pitted. In severe cases, the pox ran together and the skin looked as if it had been scorched by fire, giving this terrible disease its alternative name, the *Red Death*. The blisters could even appear on the tongue and inside the mouth and throat. When they formed on the cornea of the eyes, the patient became permanently blind.

The disease was so prevalent in Europe that there was a German saying "From love and smallpox but few remain free." The Red Death then travelled to the New World with the early Europeans. Smallpox swept like wild fire up and down the trade routes of North America, killing thousands, probably millions of members of the First Nations, including many who had never even seen a European.

No one understood yet how the loathsome disease was transmitted, but during epidemics, people with the disease were often placed in separate smallpox hospitals. During the epidemic in her area, Marie-Henriette had a cabin built in the woods where she looked after smallpox patients. Everyone who suffered from the disease looked so hideous that mirrors were not allowed in smallpox hospitals. As the pox burst open or bled, they gave off a sickening smell. Smallpox was a horror for patient and healer alike, and there was no cure for this red death that killed 40 percent of its victims.

The smallpox virus was so contagious that the disease could be transmitted on the breath of smallpox victims, in the pus that soaked their clothes and sheets, and even in the dried scabs that fell off their bodies. One case could quickly develop into an epidemic. Marie-Henriette, a determined woman with great energy, was not content with tending to smallpox victims. She also took steps to protect those in the community who had not yet caught the terrible disease.

LADY MARY'S LEGACY

Lady Mary Wortley Montagu was the brilliant wife of the British Ambassador to Turkey. While in Turkey, Lady Mary learned that the Turks protected themselves against smallpox by a procedure known as inoculation. The patient's skin was scratched with a needle that had been either rolled in a fresh smallpox scab or dipped into a smallpox blister. A small blister would form where the skin had been scratched, and nine days later the patient would have a slight rash and mild fever with few or no pox. After that, the patient was immune to smallpox or, at worst, would only suffer from a mild case of the disease.

Lady Mary daringly had her son inoculated in Turkey. When she returned to Britain in 1718, she had her young daughter inoculated as well. Lady Mary then convinced the most powerful mother in the land, the Princess of Wales, to have her children inoculated. It immediately became the fashion to have the procedure done, and smallpox gradually disappeared from Britain. Inoculation was an important step in the fight against smallpox. The disease, however, continued to rage in other European countries where the inhabitants knew about, but were suspicious of, inoculation.

Lady Mary herself, once famous for her beauty as well as her brains, was not helped by inoculation, for she had caught smallpox before she travelled to Turkey. Her face had been ravaged, but her intelligence was not affected, nor was her wish to protect others from the disease that killed as many as 60 million people in the 1700s. By being open-minded enough to see the worth of inoculation, and by cleverly convincing the Princess of Wales to approve it, Lady Mary left a valuable legacy.

The procedure was eventually imported to North America. When smallpox broke out in Cape Breton, Marie-Henriette not only tended the ill, but was also able to inoculate many people in the area.

THE RIGHT TO HEAL

Around 1802, Marie-Henriette and her family moved to Cape Breton's North East Margaree River Valley. They were early European settlers in the area, and Marie-Henriette lived the life of a pioneer. This petite, blue-eyed woman shot and killed a bear that tried to attack her in the woods. When she found a second one attacking their pig, she is reported to have killed it in the pigpen with a large fire shovel.

Marie-Henriette also continued to work as a healer and midwife for the English and French settlers in the area, as these skills were highly valued in any community. Apart from mishaps such as burns and wounds, the settlers of early Nova Scotia also suffered from diseases such as tuberculosis, diphtheria and cholera. Marie-Henriette herself lost two of her four children during infancy.

She was fortunate to live at a time in North America when her right to heal was not yet questioned because she was a woman. In Europe, by the time of the witch-hunts, males had already established a stranglehold on medicine in the cities by excluding women from medical schools. Male medical students spent most of their time studying ancient Greek philosophers and the Christian religion. There was no scientific experimentation, and medical students rarely saw patients. Ingredients such as sulphuric acid, arsenic, lead and mercury in doctors' remedies sometimes did more harm than the ailment they were supposed to cure. Blood-letting was a procedure doctors often used, even in the case of wounds. Other remedies prescribed by the university-trained doctors included eating a small portion of a grated human skull with food to prevent fits, and writing "In the name of the Father, the Son and the Holy Ghost, Amen" on a patient's jaw to stop a toothache. One doctor suggested that the inside of the stomach should be "brushed out" by drinking a glass of water containing fifty *live* millipedes, twice a day.

Although female healers were not allowed to attend and study at the universities, rural people often went to wise women for treatment. The doctors were outraged by this female competition, and the Church took their side. During the witch-hunting frenzy of the Middle Ages, the Church declared, "If a woman dare to cure *without having studied* she is a witch and must die." Since women were not allowed to study medicine at university, this meant that any female healer would be declared a "witch" if she healed another person.

Doctors were then asked to determine whether certain women were "witches." Placed in a legal position to destroy their competition, they did so, and few women healers escaped the flames. Thousands of women, whose only "sin" was to help ailing human beings, were tortured and executed during this time. By the end of the witch hunts, the male domination of medicine in Europe was almost complete.

It was different in North America, however. In the early 1800s, few university-trained doctors immigrated from Europe, and there were few medical schools in North America. As well, in rural areas, settlement was so spread out that it was difficult for doctors to make a living. Midwives and female healers, on the other hand, were already community members and their right to heal was not questioned. These women often lived on farms and did not expect to support themselves by tending the ill.

2.3 Mother and child: Inuit

Rural female healers did not view their skills as a career or as an exclusive profession. Sometimes they were paid for their services, but healing was still viewed largely as an act of compassion for another member of the community. They generally did not view the skills of healing and midwifery as hoarded knowledge that could be bought and sold like a bag of flour.

"IN HER PAINFUL AND PERILOUS HOUR"

Marie-Henriette travelled to her patients on foot, on horseback and on snowshoes. When she travelled at night, she carried a pine torch to light her way. Known for her energy and her love of adventure, Marie-Henriette did not mind a hundred-kilometre trek even in middle age.

2.4 Mother and child: Assiniboine

2.5 Mother and child: Montreal, 1898.

Marie-Henriette was a practising midwife at a time when settlers viewed any birth in the community as a women's social event. Female relatives and neighbours, as well as the midwife, gathered at the house of a woman who had gone into labour. They helped the pregnant woman by cooking meals and cleaning the house. Sometimes they held weaving or knitting or quilting bees at the house to produce diapers, clothing or blankets for the expected baby. This was "turnabout" help that the family would later repay by helping at other births, or at house or barn raisings in the community.

Some women stayed beside the midwife as observers and helpers so that they themselves could one day become midwives. Sometimes a young woman would begin to learn the craft of midwifery by helping her own mother give birth to younger brothers and sisters.

In the days when Marie-Henriette was a midwife, the main characteristic of childbirth, except in particularly isolated areas, was that the woman giving birth was surrounded by women she knew. These women reached out and supported her "in her Painful and Perilous Hour," as it was described, because childbirth was an important community event; without successful childbirth, the community would die out in a single generation.

HIGH ESTEEM

Marie-Henriette's community held her in high esteem, and even when she was quite old she continued her work as healer and midwife. Her husband, James, died in 1825, but "Granny Ross" lived and worked for another thirty-five years. Her own health must have been exceptional. Bent with age, she would still wade across a river and walk ten kilometres to her granddaughter's house. Even when Marie-Henriette became blind, she continued her work in the community. In the winter she was taken to her patients by sled; in the summer her family used a type of wheelbarrow as transport.

Midwifery continued to be legal in Nova Scotia until after the First World War, so Marie-Henriette did not live to see the "boys with the bag," as one Manitoba midwife called physicians, forcefully take over the role of community midwife.

Admired for her courage and revered for her medical expertise, Granny Ross, healer and midwife, died at the age of ninety-seven. She lived at a time when a woman's worth was measured by her skills and by her service to the community. The stories of her feats and adventures have become a part of Nova Scotia folk history.

Further suggested reading on women and healing:

Ehrenreich, Barbara and Deirdre English. *For Her Own Good*. New York: Anchor Books Doubleday, 1978.

Bennett, Jennifer. *Lilies of the Hearth*. Camden East, Ontario: Camden House Publishing, 1991.

Mason, Jutta. "A History of Midwifery in Canada," In *Report of the Task Force on the Implementation of Midwifery in Ontario*. Toronto, 1987.

CHAPTER 3

AUTHOR

EMILY SHAW BEAVAN
———— (b. circa 1820) ————

Here woman's empire is within, and here she shines the household star of the poor man's hearth; not in idleness, for in [North] America ... prosperity depends on female industry.

— Emily Beavan

The night was bitterly cold and the northern lights danced in the sky, casting down shades of red, then blue, then green. Emily knew that using the river was dangerous, but the sleighs made good time on the ice at night.

The sleighs, which were following a path across the ice, came to a sudden halt. One of the men wanted to strike out across unmarked ice to reach the shore. "Don't go," the others warned. "The ice may be unsafe in that direction." "I'll be fine," he shouted back, "and I'll be home before you!"

The man's horse bounded forward, and Emily and the others watched his sleigh head for the shore. There was a crash, followed quickly by a loud cracking noise. Horse, sleigh and driver plunged through the ice, and vanished.

MISSING PIECES

Little is known about the life of Emily Shaw Beavan. Her father was Captain Samuel Shaw, who sailed his ship between Belfast, Ireland, and Saint John, New Brunswick. It is likely that Emily was born in Belfast, but her year of birth is not known.

About 1836, Emily came to the British colony of New Brunswick, where she was a student and later a teacher. In June 1838, she married Dr. Frederick Beavan, who practised medicine in the colony, and went to live with him at English Settlement, in Queens County. While there, Emily wrote stories and poetry that were published in New Brunswick's first literary magazine. As was the custom of the day for female authors and poets, her magazine contributions were modestly signed "Mrs. B—n."

Emily also recorded her careful observations of settler life that were later published in England as a book entitled *Sketches and Tales Illustrative of Life in the backwoods of New Brunswick*. Although there is

3.1 Emily was a school teacher in New Brunswick sometime after 1836. This painting portrays another young Maritime teacher as she persuades the school trustees to buy books for her students.

little personal information about Emily in *Sketches and Tales*, the book contains a wealth of information about life in New Brunswick's pioneer settlements. Emily used a wild goose quill pen and ink made from boiled "white maple bark" to write at least part of this lively account.

THE LAND OF STRANGERS

Emily describes New Brunswick as "the land of strangers" because of its large number of immigrants. Early French settlers in the colony, known as Acadians, were later joined by United Empire Loyalists. These were people who had remained loyal to Britain during the American Revolution and who had left the newly created United States in order to continue to live under British rule. Emily sometimes refers to them and their descendants as "bluenoses" and to the colony as "America." She reports that the Loyalists referred to themselves as "Britishers."

By the time Emily arrived in New Brunswick, there were few actual Loyalists still alive. Their children and grandchildren, however, lived in settlements about the colony.

Once the Napoleonic Wars ended in Europe in 1815, there followed other great waves of immigration to the area. The inexpensive or even free land that was available in British colonies such as New Brunswick attracted many desperate people from across the Atlantic Ocean. In Ireland, there were devastating crop failures. In Scotland, families that rented and worked small farms were forced from their homes by the large landowners who wanted the land for sheep grazing. At the same time, Britain could now greatly reduce its military strength; many British officers and their families could not survive in Britain on half-pay from the army.

Emily's *Sketches and Tales* was no doubt written to inform future British immigrants about the type of life they could expect to have in the settlements of New Brunswick. The book also reveals that each immigrant group brought its own unique traditions to the colony.

HOME SWEET HOME

One of the homes Emily describes in her book was that of a friend and neighbour, Stephen Morris, who had emigrated years earlier from England. It was a typical log house with a shingled roof, two large rooms on the ground floor, and a covered porch running across the front. Outside, a hop vine was carefully trained around one of the windows to imitate the climbing roses of Morris's English homeland. Beds, complete with "old but well-cared-for" bed curtains, stood in the dark corners of one of the rooms.

The dairy was at one end of the house and the "workshop" was at the other. Emily points out that a workshop was useful because settlers had to be their own carpenters and blacksmiths.

Other neighbours, the Gordons, had immigrated from the highlands of Scotland. Emily admired Mrs. Gordon and often visited the white frame Gordon house, which stood high on a hill and was still joined to the original log cabin. The Gordon house also served as the school and church

3.2 Home sweet log home. Log City, New Brunswick, 1875.

3.3 Home sweet log home. Content, Alberta, 1908.

for the settlement. In Mrs. Gordon's parlour, the book-case stood in the place of honour, and she treasured the few books that lined its shelves.

Emily also describes the log house of Sybel and Melancthon Grey, a young married couple who were both children of Loyalists. There was no gate in the wooden fence around the Grey house, so Emily had to climb over the fence in her long skirts in order to reach it. She cheerfully indicates that once you had climbed the fence a number of times, it could be done "most gracefully." The Grey house had only one room on the ground floor, which served as both kitchen and parlour for the couple and their two young children.

The space on the second floor served as the bedroom and the storage room for items such as lumber. Emily noted that there were no bed

3.4 Home sweet log home. East of Sugarloaf, Northwest Territories, 1912.

curtains, for bluenose settlers did not use them. There was, however, a "splendid coverlet," woven from the wool of the Grey's own sheep, spread over the "airy-looking" bed. Such a coverlet was not only useful and attractive, but was also a measure of a family's success. If the lady of the house was industrious enough to produce such a valuable coverlet, the settlement knew that the family was "getting along in the world."

Sybel Grey made butter in her own dairy, which Emily described as "a little bark-lined recess" next to the house.

MOVING DAY FROLIC

Few things were wasted in early New Brunswick settlements, especially buildings. Emily and her husband quickly discovered that the land they acquired with their house—less than half a hectare—was too small to farm. They wanted to grow potatoes, but the closest farm they could buy was over three kilometres away. However, the Beavans liked their white frame house and did not wish to leave it behind. The solution was to hold a frolic and move the house to the new farm. Whenever settlers had work to be done that required the speed or strength of many hands, the neighbours were invited to come to a frolic. New Brunswickers held frolics for building houses and barns, for ploughing, planting, hoeing, chopping and piling. Women held their own frolics for "wool-picking," and for cutting out and sewing homespun woollen clothes for the winter.

As soon as there was enough snow on the ground to form a smooth "snow road," the Beavans held their frolic. Neighbours brought their tools and their oxen. They cut down two large trees and made huge sled runners from the trunks. The house was raised from its foundations and hoisted onto the wooden runners. Sixty oxen, fastened four abreast to a long pole called "a tongue," then dragged the house along the road to its new location. Emily describes the tremendous noise along the way as chains rattled, boards groaned and oxen drivers shouted instructions. A flag, which had been attached to the roof, cheerfully fluttered as the house moved along the road.

The hostess of a frolic was expected to provide food for the workers. When outdoor work was involved, the fare was hearty and might include pot pie, roast mutton, "rum dough nuts" and pumpkin pie. At women's frolics, hot tea, "sweet cake" with stewed apples and custards were served. Emily indicates that the settlers never tired of frolics and valued them as a way to lighten their work load.

BY SLEIGH AND BY CANOE

Snow was welcomed in the early European settlements of the colony. It was easier to travel in sleighs over snowy roads and frozen rivers than it was to toil along in wagons over deeply rutted roads. Roads were often badly maintained and either covered travellers in mud or choked them with dust and swarms of insects. Winter, therefore, was the easiest time to visit family and friends.

Emily describes sleigh riding as "exhilarating." The sleigh ride was often so smooth and quiet that the horses wore bells on their necks and harnesses to warn others of their approach. Sleighing across the ice, however, was sometimes dangerous. Emily reports seeing a horse, sleigh and driver crash through the ice one night. The driver was eventually rescued, but the horse and sleigh were lost.

In the warmer weather, "river settlers" often travelled in birch bark canoes. The canoes moved swiftly and could float in shallow water, but they were easily tipped over by inexperienced travellers. Emily marvels at the small girls who paddled a "cargo" of even smaller brothers and sisters to school. She also records that even settler women with babies fearlessly paddled the useful, if easily overturned, canoes.

SPARKINGS, STUMPINGS AND WEDDINGS

Early New Brunswick settlers referred to courtship as "sparking," and Emily tells an amusing sparking tale. A young man named Leonidas van Wort wished to marry an attractive young Irish woman named Grace Marley. Grace lived with her aunt and uncle, and when Leonidas came sparking one evening, the young couple were tactfully left alone by the fireside. Grace did not like Leonidas, however, so she was delighted when the young man, unused to small talk, fell asleep in his chair. Before escaping, Grace mischievously threw a white cloth over the tall, slim butter churn standing in the room and moved it over by Leonidas's side. Then she went off to bed. The next morning Grace's uncle found Leonidas, still asleep, embracing the butter churn as if it were a slim-waisted woman. The old man's laughter woke up Leonidas, who stalked out of the house and never returned.

Emily reports that in earlier days it was the custom to announce an upcoming marriage by "stumping." The names of the intended bride and groom and the place and date of the wedding ceremony were written on pieces of paper that were stuck into the many tree stumps along the roadside. The couple were married by the local "squire" who read the wedding ceremony from the prayer book and received one dollar as his pay.

By the time Emily came to New Brunswick, a wedding was viewed as "a regular frolic" and the ceremony was usually performed by a clergyman in front of a large crowd of people.

It appears that both bride and groom were expected to contribute items to their new household. Sybel Grey's "bridal portion" had been a cow,

3.5 When Grace Marley played a trick on her love-struck suitor, she used a butter churn similar to the one pictured here.

some sheep and a few household articles such as a bake pan and a tea kettle. Melancthon Grey had contributed molasses, tea, a barrel of pork and a barrel of flour. Emily's detailed account in *Sketches and Tales* of her visit to this young couple's home is both touching and charming.

AT HOME IN THE BACKWOODS

The only room on the ground floor of the Greys' log house contained a pine table and "willow-seated" chairs that had been made in the area. The baby slept in a cradle while the older child played with the rocking chair or with bark and chips of wood which were the only "toys" in the house. For decoration, a reticule (small bag) decorated with porcupine quills and a pair of beaded moccasins were hung on the bare wooden walls. "Indian baskets," woven in bright colours, were piled up on top of each other. A rifle hung over the fireplace, where the warmth of the fire would keep its metal from rusting. A store-bought wooden "Yankee clock" sat in the room, but Sybel preferred to use the sun mark cut into the floor as a guide for timing the noon meal.

Corn cobs hung from the rafters to provide seed for the next year's crop. Also hanging from the rafters was the family's supply of herbs and roots, gathered from the local woods and fields. Among the carefully stored plants, Emily noticed sage, savory, boneset, lobelia, sarsaparilla, catnip, calamus root, balm of Gilead buds and dried marigold leaves. Some of the stored plants were used to flavour food and some were used for dying cloth. Others had healing properties which the settlers had learned about from the people of the First Nations. The only books in the house were a Bible, an almanac (a type of calendar) and a book of sacred music.

In the room upstairs, "snow white blankets" were piled on a large chest beside the bed. There were no closets, so the family's homemade woollen garments were hung around the walls of the room.

DINNER IN THE BACKWOODS

At noon, Sybel called Melancthon home for his dinner by blowing their horn. The horn was a conch shell with a hole bored in the one end and its sound travelled a great distance. Emily reports that the cheerful sound of noontime horns could be heard from settlement to settlement. The same sound at night, however, signalled trouble. Sometimes a desperate family blew its horn to guide a lost member home from the forest. Sometimes the night sounding of a horn meant that a house was on fire and the family was calling for help.

Emily's noon meal with Sybel and Melancthon was a typical hot weather dinner in New Brunswick. They ate fresh trout from the nearby stream, fried ham, potatoes, fresh beans, and salad with home-made vinegar. There was also a large "hot cake" made from corn meal, milk and dried blueberries, and "buscuits" made from "Tenessee flour," cream and "sal-a-ratus." Sal-a-ratus (potassium bicarbonate) was used in place of yeast to make batter rise. Settlers could buy it at the general store or make it at home by dissolving wood ashes in water and then evaporating the liquid. The Greys ended their summer dinner with raspberry pie, a dish of strawberries and cream and the hot tea that was drunk with every New Brunswick meal.

WOMEN'S WORK IN THE BACKWOODS

Emily indicates that the most important part of women's work was the "manufacture" of wool produced by each farm's flock of sheep. Women brought the wool to the carding mill, sometimes by canoe. There, for a price, the wool was combed until all the fibres were brushed straight. It was then twisted into soft balls and returned to the women ready for spinning. At home the wool was placed on the point of the spindle of a spinning wheel, spun into yarn and then wound into lengths called skeins. Sybel Grey hung her skeins on poles outside the house to bleach in the sun. Some wool was dyed with butternut bark or "sweet fern" or indigo to give it colour.

Emily notes that the wool in Sybel's homespun dress was carded, spun, dyed and woven into a pretty plaid by the industrious Sybel, who had also cut and sewn the cloth. Around her neck, Sybel wore "a bright gingham handkerchief" tucked inside her dress. Emily also approves of the fact that Sybel did not hide her hair under a cap but wore neat braids instead. The backwoods settlers wore their rawhide moccasins and homespun, homemade clothing with pride. They viewed expensive "boughten" clothing as a sign that the wearer was a poor manager and probably in debt.

Emily's neighbours had differing views on whether or not women should work in the fields. Mrs. Stephen Morris had been accustomed to working outdoors in England. In New Brunswick she toiled alongside her husband clearing, fencing, planting and reaping. The bluenoses, however, considered that it was "agin all nature" for a woman to work in the fields. Sybel Grey, therefore, had the pale complexion of a woman who worked indoors.

MORE MISSING PIECES

Sketches and Tales is full of detailed and sometimes surprising images like these, of early settler life in New Brunswick. Emily's account of the spicy scent of cedar that clung to the cows when they returned home from the cedar woods is wonderfully vivid. Her description of bloated "musquitoes" clinging wearily to the walls after a night of feasting on sleeping settlers is timeless.

In the spring of 1843, Emily left for Ireland with her husband and never returned. *Sketches and Tales* was published in England in 1845, but nothing more is known about its author.

Why did she leave New Brunswick? Did she have any children? Was her life a happy one? When and where did she die? All these many pieces are missing from the mosaic of Emily's life. *Sketches and Tales* gives the reader an all too brief look at the life and times of author Emily Shaw Beavan.

Further suggested reading:

Beavan, Mrs. F. *Sketches and Tales Illustrative of Life in the backwoods of New Brunswick,* London: George Routledge, 1845. Reprinted. St. Stephen, New Brunswick: Print'n Press Publications Ltd., 1980.

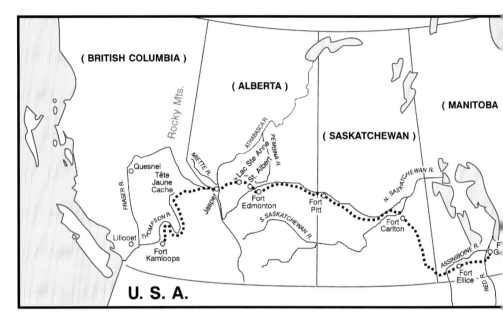

TREK OF THE OVERLANDERS IN 1862

CHAPTER 4

OVERLANDER

CATHERINE O'HARE SCHUBERT

(1835-1918)

A brave and notable pioneer.

—Monument honouring Catherine Schubert

The horse, Buck, hesitated at the water's edge, reluctant to tackle another rain-swollen river. In the saddle sat Catherine Schubert, exhausted and six months pregnant. One child was tied to her back so he could not be swept away by the rushing water.

Just as Catherine leaned forward to urge Buck on, the horse threw back his head. He hit Catherine in the face with such force that one of her teeth was knocked out. Waves of pain swept over her, but there was no turning back.

Blood streaming from her aching mouth, Catherine finally crossed the Pembina River. As the angry water swirled around her, she prayed they would reach the Cariboo in time.

AMERICA

Catherine O'Hare, the youngest of nine children, was born in Ireland in 1835. At age sixteen, she sailed to the United States and worked as a maid for a wealthy family in Springfield, Massachusetts. She used her few spare hours to teach herself to read.

When Catherine was nineteen, she met a twenty-seven-year-old German carpenter named Augustus Schubert. He was a hard-working, hot-tempered man who dreamed of becoming rich. Catherine married Augustus in 1855 and they moved to St. Paul, on the Mississippi River.

PIG'S EYE AND FORT GARRY

St. Paul, the bustling capital of the Minnesota Territory, was an important trading post that had once been named Pig's Eye. Catherine opened a grocery store in St. Paul and sold her home-made bread, while Augustus worked as a carpenter. Their son Gus was born in 1856 and their daughter Mary Jane was born in 1858. That year, however, a depression hit the area and Augustus could no longer find work. In the dead of winter, Catherine and her family packed themselves and their possessions into horse-drawn sleighs. They travelled 900 kilometres through forests and across frozen, windswept plains to start a new life in Fort Garry (now Winnipeg, Manitoba).

Fort Garry was located on the Red River in the vast area known as Rupert's Land, which was controlled by the Hudson's Bay Company. Catherine and Augustus bought a farm, set up a store, and joined the many Métis (people with both First Nations and French ancestors) and retired Hudson's Bay employees living in the Red River settlement. Jimmy, Catherine's third child, was born in 1860.

The Schuberts lost their farm and their store in the devastating spring floods of 1862. They were just beginning to rebuild in late May when strangers arrived in Fort Garry who would change Catherine's life forever.

GOLD AND THE OVERLANDERS OF '62

In 1858, miners had discovered gold dust and nuggets in the lower reaches of the Fraser River, in what is now the province of British Columbia. The miners believed that somewhere along the Fraser was "the mother lode"—the main vein that was the source of those bits of gold carried downstream by the river. They pushed farther and farther up the Fraser and its tributaries, searching for the precious yellow metal. In late 1859, they discovered gold on the Quesnel River, in the Cariboo Mountains, and by 1860 there were 4000 prospectors searching the many creeks of the Quesnel area. News of the rich gold fields spread; in the spring of 1862, people from all over the world rushed to "the fabulous Cariboo" to seek their fortune.

Most gold-seekers travelled up the Pacific coast by boat. In 1859, however, three small groups from the East had reached the gold fields by following fur trade routes that led west across the prairies and over the Rocky Mountains.

On 26 May 1862, 150 men arrived by paddle-steamer at Fort Garry determined to follow the "overland" route to the Cariboo. The Overlanders, as they became known, consisted of fifteen smaller groups of gold-seekers who had met as they travelled west. At Fort Garry, they were joined by another group of 50, who arrived by ox-cart.

Catherine's husband, Augustus, always anxious for quick riches, decided to join the Overlanders and go search for gold in the Cariboo. No matter how much Catherine argued, Augustus refused to consider taking his family along. Catherine, however, had no intention of being left behind to run the farm and the store and care for their three small children alone.

4.1 One of the Overlanders was artist William Hind. This is his water-colour of the Overlanders setting out from Fort Garry with their Red River carts.

THE JOURNEY BEGINS

As it turned out, Catherine could be as persuasive as she was determined. In spite of the fact that the Overlanders had a "men only" rule, she went to the leader of the expedition and talked him into letting her and the children go with Augustus. The Overlanders were predicting that it would take two months to travel to the gold fields, and Catherine was careful not to mention that she was already four months pregnant. If the trip took only two months, she would be settled in the Cariboo long before her fourth child was born.

When Catherine told Augustus that she and the children were coming, he ended the argument as he ended all arguments. He hurled dishes at the wall and left in a rage. Eventually, he calmed down and found a buyer for their store and farm. Catherine quickly sold most of their belongings and bought provisions for the long trip ahead. The group would push west through Rupert's Land from one tiny, isolated Hudson's Bay fort or post to the next, and could not rely on others for food along the way.

On June 2, 1862, the Overlanders set off from Fort Garry. Catherine rode her horse with large straw baskets slung on either side of the animal. In one basket sat Gus, not yet six, and in the other sat three-year-old Mary Jane. Augustus carried Jimmy, who was not yet two. A cow and an ox pulled their wagon. The Schuberts' two hired hands had decided to join the expedition, and they looked after the other cows and horses.

The entire group, consisting of some 200 people, 97 carts and 110 animals, stretched almost a kilometre across the land. No one was aware of the difficult swamps, dense forests, raging rivers and treacherous mountain paths that lay ahead of them on the 3000-kilometre trail. On a good day the group could travel 32 kilometres, but there would be few good days for the Overlanders of '62.

4.2 William Hind's water-colour shows the Overlanders on a duck hunt; their wagons are in the distance. Hind made over 160 sketches or water-colours between Fort Garry and the Rocky Mountains.

BUG BITES AND BUFFALO DROPPINGS

During the first stage of the trip, the Overlanders rose at four in the morning and set out an hour later. They travelled until eleven, then again from two to six. The group rarely travelled on Sundays. Whenever they stopped, some of the men tried to fish or hunt; others saw to various chores and then rested. Catherine, however, with three children under the age of six to care for and keep amused, rarely had a chance to rest.

On the way to Fort Ellice, the group had had to lower animals and wagons down steep river banks, build bridges across, then haul the animals and wagons up the other side. One river bank was a hill of shifting

40

sand which Catherine, in her long, cumbersome skirts, crawled up on her hands and knees.

The Overlanders arrived at Fort Ellice on June 14, then headed northwest toward Fort Carlton. As they travelled, clouds of black flies and mosquitoes descended upon humans and animals alike, stinging and biting without mercy. After they struggled across the Qu'Appelle River, with its 150-metre-high banks, their guide stole a rifle and deserted.

Undaunted, the Overlanders continued to trudge across the vast prairies. Wood was scarce, so they collected dried buffalo droppings to use as fuel for their cooking fires. The June sun beat down upon the grasslands, and one horse dropped dead of heat exhaustion. To avoid moving in the merciless afternoon heat, the group changed their travelling hours to very early morning and late evening. Worried about horse thieves, they drew the wagons into a huge triangle at night. Animals and humans slept inside the triangle while armed guards stood watch.

RAGING RIVERS AND HUNGRY DOGS

After Fort Carlton, the Overlanders crawled through a blinding sandstorm for two hours until they reached grasslands. They worried about being caught in the middle of one of the battles between the Blackfoot and Cree, who were constantly at war with each other. A pack of wolves trailed them to Fort Pitt, and kept the nervous group awake at night with their howls.

New problems awaited after Fort Pitt. There was heavy, almost constant rain for eleven days. The Overlanders as well as all their clothing, tents and food were soaked. Catherine frantically fed her children herbal broth and rubbed goose grease on their chests to keep them from catching pneumonia. By day, the group sloshed along, miserably pushing carts through grasslands that had turned into seas of mud. By night, the tents leaked and it was impossible to keep fires going long enough to dry anything out. Overlanders who kept diaries noted that even inside the tents they were up to their ankles in water.

The endless rains caused the streams and rivers that zigzagged across the prairies to swell. The Overlanders waded or swam across many raging torrents that were over a metre deep. Some of the rain-swollen rivers and streams, however, were too large or dangerous for wading. In the space of three days, the group had to build eight bridges, ranging in length from twelve metres to thirty, with only the materials they found around them. Sometimes animals and carts had to be hauled, one by one, up and down the steep sides of ravines.

When the Overlanders finally staggered into Fort Edmonton, the Hudson's Bay officials there told them that such a large group should not attempt to cross the Rocky Mountains so late in the year. Some members

4.3 During Catherine's lifetime many other women began the westward journey. These homesteaders are on the move in 1905.

4.4 Like Catherine, many women began their travels full of hope. Here, a honeymoon couple are on their way to their Alberta homestead in 1914.

of the party decided to stay in Edmonton, but most, including Catherine and her family, were determined to push on to the Cariboo. As they made preparations to leave, they were plagued by the five or six hundred stray dogs that lived around the fort. Some Overlanders took to sleeping on top

4.5 Catherine and the other Overlanders of 1862 were often forced to wade or swim across turbulent streams and rivers. The homesteaders seen here in 1910 are able to cross the Peace River by boat.

of their supply of pemmican (a type of dried buffalo meat) to keep the bold animals from stealing their food. On the advice of the Hudson's Bay officials, the Overlanders traded their carts for pack horses to use on the narrow trails ahead. They also hired a Métis guide who agreed to lead the expedition as far as Tête Jaune Cache in the Rocky Mountains. When they left Fort Edmonton on July 29, the Overlanders had already travelled 1600 difficult kilometres in two months. The worst, however, was yet to come.

SWAMPS AND MORE SWAMPS

After passing St. Albert and Lac Ste Anne, the Overlanders had to chop a narrow trail through dense forest. Catherine put Gus on her horse and, although six months pregnant, carried three-year-old Mary Jane on her back. On August 6, the Overlanders swam their horses across the turbulent waters of the Pembina River. Once across the river, they struggled on foot through swampland. The legs of their horses completely disappeared into the cold, sticky mud. Some Overlanders left their animals behind to die in the swamps, but most used logs to pry out the exhausted, kicking animals. After three large swamps, it took another eight days to struggle through a series of smaller ones.

By now, the days were getting shorter, the land was rising, and the nights were cold. The heavy dew sometimes froze overnight.

ROCKY MOUNTAIN HORROR

Finally, the Overlanders came in sight of the Rocky Mountains. They had earlier decided to follow the route through Tête Jaune Pass (also known as Yellowhead or Leather Pass) up to the headwaters of the Fraser River; it was the quickest route and they were worried about their dwindling food supplies. Tête Jaune Pass, however, was also the most dangerous route, with trails that were almost impassable. The Overlanders began to climb the mountain trail past Jasper and over the Rocky Mountains sometime around August 20. Near the top of the steep trail, the group was attacked by hornets. Most were stung and Catherine's children screamed in pain.

Further along, the trail became a narrow ledge with a sheer drop on one side and a rock wall on the other. Two pack horses slipped over the edge and fell to their death. Catherine's children, however, safely wriggled along the narrow ledge on their stomachs.

The trail, no more than thirty centimetres wide, then zigzagged down between jagged rocks and crossed a turbulent, thirty-metre-wide stream that swept around huge boulders. On the other side of the stream, the path again moved steeply upward. Catherine, now seven months pregnant, was chilled by the cold mountain air and her leg and back muscles stiffened in protest. But there could be no turning back. That night, the hungry group killed and ate one of the oxen.

The trail then climbed up a steep, pebble-strewn slope. The animals had to be hauled up by ropes, and Catherine and her children scrambled up on their hands and knees.

After rafting across the Athabasca River, the Overlanders came to a burned-out forest, choked with hundreds of fallen trees. Pushing onward, the group had to cross and recross the icy Miette River seven times in two hours to reach Tête Jaune Pass.

As they pushed through the pass in the centre of the Rocky Mountains, the Overlanders could manage only about sixteen kilometres per day. Even at that slow pace, they were too tired and terrified to enjoy the magnificent scenery that surrounded them. Beyond the pass, the trail zigzagged up and down a steep mountainside. Ice-fed streams formed waterfalls across it, and Catherine and two others clung together as they stumbled through or under the bone-chilling, thundering waters.

By August 22, the Overlanders reached The Great Divide and the headwaters of the Fraser River. At this point the rivers began to rush down the mountains, not toward the east but westward, toward the Pacific Ocean. They were close to starvation. Along the trail Catherine and her family ate squirrel, skunk and even one of their exhausted pack horses. The first night in British Columbia, Catherine, the first European woman to enter British Columbia overland from eastern Canada, made dinner out of some black, hairy moss boiled with lichens and huckleberries.

The next day, the Overlanders travelled along a narrow ledge high above the Fraser River. One horse slipped, fell into the churning waters below and was swept away, never to be seen again. Catherine was terrified until her children had safely snaked across the ledge on their stomachs.

TO RAFT OR NOT TO RAFT

On August 27, the exhausted Overlanders reached Tête Jaune Cache. At this point, the group split in two. Most Overlanders decided to build large rafts and travel down the perilous Fraser River to the mining town of Quesnel.

The Schuberts wanted to take this route, but the trip was so dangerous that none of the men on the rafts would allow Catherine and the children to take such a risk. Catherine and Augustus could not manage a raft down the Fraser on their own, and so they were forced to join the group of thirty Overlanders heading for Fort Kamloops on the Thompson River. This land route was safer but slower—and time was running out for Catherine.

On September 2, the Schuberts and the others taking the land route began the miserable fourteen-day trek to the Thompson River. It was exactly three months since they had left Fort Garry. They hacked their way through thick hemlock forests in a constant drizzle that sometimes turned into sleet and hail as the days grew colder. Her feet wet and swollen, Catherine carried three-year-old Mary Jane on her back through swamps, over fallen trees, up and down hills and through ferns that grew as high as their heads.

Once they reached the Thompson, the Overlanders began to hack a trail along the river. The going was painfully slow, however, and they soon realized they would never reach Fort Kamloops at this rate. They decided they would raft down the Thompson, a somewhat calmer river than the Fraser. Many had been saving their horses and oxen to use in the Cariboo gold fields, but animals could not be taken on the rafts. The animals were slaughtered and their meat smoked over wood fires to provide food for the long trip down the Thompson.

The Schuberts made a dugout canoe out of a cedar tree and packed it the day before their departure with their food and extra clothing. During the night, however, disaster struck. The river's powerful current quietly carried the canoe away, and the Schuberts awoke to find that all they had left was their tents, their blankets and the clothes they were wearing. Other Overlanders helped as best they could, but such a large food loss nearly cost the Schuberts their lives.

NIGHTMARE ON THE THOMPSON

The trip down the Thompson was grim. At one point Catherine and the others were forced to portage around some dangerous rapids. Without animals to help carry the loads over the rough country, the fourteen-kilometre trip took three days. It also began to snow. At the end of the portage the Schuberts built a raft and set off again. The raft spun around in the turbulent waters and wedged itself on some rocks. It remained there for two hours before breaking apart. The Schuberts managed to wade to shore through the icy water with the children and the tents. They built a new raft and set out again, this time staying close to the shore so they could try to shoot birds or small animals for food.

As the Schuberts poled the raft along the remaining 200 kilometres downriver, icy winds chilled them to the bone. Sometimes it snowed and they could not see the way. When they ran out of ammunition, they lived on hazelnuts, huckleberries, thimble berries and even wild rose hips that they gathered along the way. The children shivered and cried with cold and hunger. On October 7, the desperate Schuberts approached a First Nations village for food. To their horror, they discovered only rotting corpses; the entire village had been wiped out by a smallpox epidemic. Catherine and Augustus hastily dug potatoes out of the village garden then fled the place in dread. They lived on the raw potatoes for three or four days.

Still floating down the Thompson on October 14, Catherine went into labour on the raft. Augustus took her ashore to a Shuswap village and begged for help. When the women saw that Catherine was about to give birth, they took control of the situation. Under their kind care, she gave birth to a healthy girl, whom she named Rose, after the wild rose hips the family had eaten to stay alive.

HOME IN BRITISH COLUMBIA

The Shuswap village was near Fort Kamloops and the Schuberts finished their journey a few days later. They spent a year at the fort, working as carpenter and cook. In 1863, Catherine and Augustus bought a farm near Lillooet, on the main road to the Cariboo. There was no school in the area, so Catherine, who believed strongly in the value of education, taught the local children in her home for free.

Augustus never truly rid himself of gold fever, and over the years he travelled back and forth to the gold fields, never with much success. Catherine became a business woman and supported her family by running her own road house, or hotel, as well as the farm. Most European women in the Cariboo supported themselves and their families by running hotels, saloons, restaurants, laundries or boarding houses for the thousands of miners in the area.

At one point Augustus persuaded Catherine to move the family to Quesnel, to be closer to him and the gold fields. Again, she supported the family by setting up a restaurant. Quesnel, however, was a dangerous town, full of desperate and starving miners, and there were frequent armed robberies. After two years, Catherine took the children back to live in their hotel in Lillooet.

Some years and another son and daughter later, Catherine sold the hotel and accepted the position of matron for fifty girls at a Cache Creek boarding school. Taking her two youngest children with her, she taught domestic science at the school and looked after the girls when they were ill. While she was there, her daughter Mary Jane, whom Catherine had carried on her back over the Overland Trail, died of tuberculosis in Winnipeg, leaving a husband and young children behind.

In 1881, Augustus swore his gold-hunting days were over and bought a farm in British Columbia's Okanagan Valley. Once the land was cleared and a house was built, Catherine gave up her job at the Cache Creek school and joined her husband. The land was rich, and once again Catherine set up a road house for the stage coaches that passed through the area.

Whenever a new settler appeared, Catherine dropped off a basket of groceries and her own baking. She also delighted in teaching the young women how to preserve food and how to make soap and candles. Never losing her belief in the value of education, Catherine talked Augustus into donating a piece of land for a local school.

To the end, Augustus continued with his hot-tempered, plate-throwing ways. Whenever he drove into the village for groceries, Catherine always included an order for new dishes.

Augustus died in 1908 and Catherine sold the farm and moved into nearby Armstrong. She remained a vital part of the community until her death on 18 July 1918, at the age of eighty-three.

In 1926, Armstrong erected a large, granite monument in honour of Catherine O'Hare Schubert, an outstanding pioneer and an extraordinary woman.

Further suggested reading:

Metcalf, Vicky. *Catherine Schubert*. Toronto: Fitzhenry & Whiteside Limited, 1978.

5.1 Frances Anne Hopkins in 1863

CHAPTER 5

ARTIST

FRANCES ANNE HOPKINS
—— (1838 - 1919) ——

I have not found Canadians at all anxious hitherto for pictures of their own country.

— Frances Anne Hopkins, 1910

A man and a young woman stood in front of a large oil painting of a canoe plunging into rapids. The birchbark canoe and its passengers seemed to leap toward the viewer.

"You must put this foolish nonsense of becoming a painter out of your head, my dear," the man grumbled. "It is well known that women simply do not have the intelligence or the talent for art. Only a man can be an artist. Besides, your friends make pictures out of feathers and glue seashells on boxes. Why can't you be happy doing that?"

The young woman sighed. "Because I want to paint. And you have seen my paintings, Papa. Everyone says they are good."

"Yes, well, but not like this new exhibition piece," he replied, pointing his walking stick toward the painting of the canoe. "This piece is bold. The colours are fresh and vivid. And look at those rapids. This artist really understands the way water moves. Extraordinary, really," he added thoughtfully.

"I'm sorry my dear," he patted his daughter's hand, "but you could never paint like this. You're a woman. A woman can't be an artist because it ... it just isn't natural."

"Who is the artist, anyway?" he demanded. "I'd like to meet the chap."

His daughter glanced down at the London Royal Academy catalogue in her hand, then looked up with a delighted smile. "The painting is called Shooting the Rapids, and ... " she paused triumphantly, "the artist, dearest Papa, is a woman. Her name is Frances Anne Hopkins."

ACCOMPLISHMENT ART

Often books and articles dealing with North American history are illustrated by pictures such as *Shooting the Rapids* or *Canoe Manned by Voyageurs Passing a Waterfall* or *Voyageurs at Dawn*. As a result, these images are vaguely familiar to most Canadians. Few realize that the artist was a woman.

Frances Anne Beechey was born in England in 1838, the third daughter in a family of five girls. The family was a distinguished one, for Frances' grandfather, Sir William Beechey, was a well-known portrait painter and her grandmother was an expert painter of miniatures. Her father, Rear-admiral Frederick Beechey, was an Arctic explorer and a talented artist as well.

It is likely that Frances' education as a young, upper-class female in Victorian England would have included art lessons. Young ladies received basic art lessons in their homes or in schools from governesses or drawing masters. Being able to sketch or to paint watercolours was considered an "accomplishment" that would make young women more "feminine" and more "ladylike." Middle- and upper-class women were expected to have considerable leisure, and "accomplishment art" was a suitable way for them to pass the time. It was not, however, suitable for a lady to make a *career* out of art.

Oil painting was not usually part of accomplishment art because it required more materials and was considered rather dirty and smelly. It was not, therefore, a suitable drawing-room activity for ladies.

As well, most women did not receive the serious training necessary to produce the large, highly finished pictures associated, at that time, with oil painting. Women, it was thought, were unable to complete large oil paintings. They were told they did not have the "strength of will and power of creation" that men did, and could not even be called "artists." In an era when a separate vocabulary was often used to describe women's work, a female who painted was referred to as a "paintress."

UNLADYLIKE

Women were also told that any work that made them noticeable outside of the home or brought them into contact with men was "unladylike." A middle- or upper-class girl was expected to become exclusively a wife, mother and lady, and her upbringing was devoted to making this her one desire. No matter how talented an artist she might be, a young lady was raised to have no ambition other than to be a modest dabbler. Art was only to be a well-bred way to pass the time.

It was also "unladylike" for a woman to take money for her work, for each of her activities was supposed to be a labour of love. Young ladies

5.2 *Canoes in a Fog, Lake Superior*, **by Frances Anne Hopkins. The attention to detail, present in all of Frances' voyageur paintings, can be seen in the distinctive dress of the young men.**

were taught that only the women of the lower classes worked to support their families. This attitude ignored reality, for some middle- and upper-class women were, in fact, forced to earn a living. Women whose husbands were dead or missing, women who did not marry, and women with financially dependent parents or children all needed to make money. Often a woman in this position had to turn to art, for it was one of the few occupations in which she had the slightest training.

ART EDUCATION FOR WOMEN

For women who dared to believe in their own creative talent or who hoped to earn a living through art, education was a problem. There were few opportunities in England for them to take the art training that moved them past the "accomplishment art" level. Women were not admitted as students into the Royal Academy of Art until three years after Frances left for Canada. The few art schools in London that did admit women offered them only limited instruction in separate "women's classes." We do not know if Frances attended any art schools, but like many Victorian families, the Beecheys did not think women should take up art as a paying career.

MARRIAGE

At the age of twenty, Frances Anne Beechey married Edward Hopkins in London, England. Edward, a thirty-eight-year-old widower with three small sons, was the private secretary of Sir George Simpson, Governor of the Hudson's Bay Company.

After the wedding, Frances travelled to Lachine, Canada East (now Quebec), to begin married life. Later, she and Edward moved to Montreal. Although Frances must have been kept busy with three stepsons and

51

eventually three children of her own, she often put her artistic talents to use in her sketchbooks.

5.3 *Canoe Manned by Voyageurs Passing A Waterfall*, **by Frances Anne Hopkins. While paintings of Canada in the 1860s often portrayed tiny figures in a huge landscape, Frances boldly focused on individuals.**

THE SKETCHBOOKS

Frances' first sketchbook, which is now in the Royal Ontario Museum in Toronto, contains thirty-six sketches in pencil or in pen and ink. As soon as she arrived in Lachine, Frances began to fill this sketchbook with the scenes that surrounded her, including the canoes and sailboats that plied the Lachine River, which flowed past their home. Some of these early sketches are complete, while others provided Frances with working material for later canvases.

A second sketchbook, dated 1865, contains a number of small finished watercolours among its fourteen images. The sketches in it provide a precise and polished record of Francis' life as a young wife in Canada.

At this point in her career, art critics would have viewed Frances as no more than a gifted accomplishment artist. Her charming sketches and small watercolours were the socially acceptable products of an English lady who was busy with small children and household duties. Only later would she paint the large, lush images known as the "voyageur paintings" that so many now associate with fur trade history.

THE FUR TRADE

In the late 1660s, the English laid claim to the huge area of North America drained by rivers that flowed into Hudson Bay. In 1670, the English king granted this vast area, known as Rupert's Land, to the Hudson's Bay Company.

5.4 *Voyageurs at Dawn*, **by Frances Anne Hopkins. At night, the voyageurs slept under the overturned canoes.**

By this time the French were well established at Quebec, and they controlled the fur trade along the St. Lawrence - Great Lakes waterway as far west as Lake Superior. In response to the competition from Hudson's Bay, French traders soon began expanding their network of posts. They pushed further west, along Lake Superior, then through the river system that led to Lake Winnipeg and, eventually, beyond. Many of the trading posts they set up were in Rupert's Land, but there was little the Hudson's Bay Company could do about it; the area was far too big to patrol effectively.

The French threat to the Hudson's Bay Company ended when France withdrew from North America in 1763. That did not mean the end of competition for the fur trade, however. Enterprising British merchants based in Montreal were soon hiring the experienced crews of voyageurs and financing expeditions along the old French routes. In time, these merchants joined forces and created the North West Company.

After years of bitter, sometimes violent rivalry, the two companies united in 1821 under the name of the Hudson's Bay Company. The reorganized company was run profitably for forty years by Sir George Simpson, the employer of Edward Hopkins. Edward was eventually put in charge of an area that stretched from Montreal to Fort William (now Thunder Bay, Ontario), and he often made long canoe trips to inspect the fur trade posts under his control. In the 1860s, Frances sometimes accompanied her husband on these tours. Sketchbook in hand, she was able to record her observations of the Canadian wilderness and the remarkable voyageurs.

THE VOYAGEURS

The flamboyant French-speaking voyageurs who paddled the company canoes from sunrise to sunset, were a fascinating group. These men, who had developed their own customs and colourful dress, were in motion much of the year. Up by 4:00 a.m., they paddled at the amazing rate of forty-five strokes a minute, often singing a lively canoe song to keep a steady pace and pass the time. Each song verse was sung as a solo with the rest of the crew (usually over twenty paddlers in two long "freight" canoes) joining in to sing the chorus.

Every two hours the voyageurs stopped for five to ten minutes to rest their arms and light their pipes. Then they set off again. At darkness, they set up camp for the night and usually ate a meal of dried peas or cornmeal boiled with water and lard.

WITNESS TO THE END OF AN ERA

Frances sketched as she travelled the fur trade routes up into Lake Nipigon and between Lachine and Fort William. For English ladies, travel by canoe was almost unheard of, yet judging by the paintings, Frances enjoyed the adventure. Later, she used her sketches to create large oil paintings to record what she had witnessed. Perhaps she realized that the voyageur way of life was about to vanish.

Railways were spreading across North America, and soon it would be easier, quicker and cheaper to move people, furs and supplies across the continent by train. As the railways arrived, old fur trade routes were abandoned and the freight canoe became an antique.

FUR TRADE DOCUMENTS

The voyageur paintings of Frances Anne Hopkins give the viewer a glimpse of the details of daily voyageur life. They show the decorated birchbark canoes, the drinking cups and cooking utensils the men used, the earrings and the brightly coloured kerchiefs and sashes they wore. These pictures are considered to be so accurate and faultless in detail that they have often been studied by historians as "documents" of fur trade life.

The voyageur paintings were unusual for their time. They do not contain the moral or highly emotional scenes so popular with Victorian audiences. As well, each person on the canvas is clearly an individual with identifiable facial features and expressions. This combination of landscape and portrait art made the voyageur paintings of Frances Anne Hopkins unique. It is interesting that she often placed herself in the paintings along with her trademark, the white waterlily. Unfortunately not all of her voyageur oil paintings can be located today.

THE VOYAGEUR PAINTINGS

Once she started painting in oil, Frances returned again and again to the fur trade scenes she had sketched, even though at that time they seemed not only "unfeminine" but also "unpaintworthy" to most people in Canada

5.5 *Canoe Party Around Campfire*, by Frances Anne Hopkins. At the end of the day, the canoes were pulled ashore and any damage was carefully repaired with hot pitch.

5.6 An X-ray of *Canoe Party Around Campfire* reveals that Frances had started the painting as a day scene with a cabin in the distance behind the canoe. By changing to a night scene, she was able to show her technical skill with the play of firelight on the figures.

and Great Britain. Yet if her choice of subject matter seemed odd to those around her, the artistic talent of Frances Hopkins was recognized during her lifetime.

It was an honour for any artist to have work accepted for exhibition in the Royal Academy in London, England. It was a particularly great honour for a woman, since the Royal Academy did not admit women into membership at that time. But "outsiders" were sometimes invited to exhibit their work.

Frances' first painting to be accepted by the Royal Academy was her oil painting *Canoes in a Fog, Lake Superior*, which was exhibited in 1869. Three canoes are shown slipping into one of the cold, eerie summer fogs so common along the north and east shores of Lake Superior. Frances, in the fashionable ladies' attire of the day, is sitting in the canoe nearest the viewer. *Canoe Manned by Voyageurs Passing a Waterfall*, the second voyageur painting, was exhibited in 1870 at the Royal Academy. This vibrant oil shows Frances and her husband in a canoe with eight paddlers. The canoe, which is painted in great detail, is moving slowly so that one of the voyageurs can gather white water lilies for Frances.

A third voyageur painting was exhibited at the Royal Academy in 1874. *Voyageurs at Dawn* describes daybreak at a voyageur campsite on a rocky beach. One of the men searches for a break in the early morning fog while the others see to their chores. *Canoe Party Around the Campfire*, which is undated, shows the end of a long day of canoeing. Some of the voyageurs are repairing the seams of the birchbark canoe with hot pitch while the others gather around the fire. A fifth voyageur painting is entitled *Shooting the Rapids* and was painted around 1879. The large canoe, with its sixteen paddlers and four passengers, is pointed almost directly at the viewer. The voyageurs are working in unison at the sternman's command. This painting is the recreation of an event in 1863 when Frances, her husband and Governor Dallas of the Hudson's Bay Company ran the Lachine Rapids in the governor's canoe. *Shooting the Rapids* boldly celebrates the individuals who worked together to span a continent by canoe.

Between 1869 and 1918 Frances had thirteen works accepted for exhibition at the Royal Academy. She also had exhibitions at the Art Association of Montreal, the Royal Society of British Artists, the Society of Women Artists and various other galleries. She was not, however, a widely known artist in her time, as the Canadian and British public showed little interest in any of her work that focused on Canadian scenery.

LARGELY UNKNOWN

When Edward resigned from the Hudson's Bay Company in 1870, the Hopkinses moved back to England. There, Frances maintained an art studio and continued to paint scenes based on the sketches and watercolours she had produced while living in Canada. After Edward died in 1893, Frances used her artistic skill to provide herself with extra income. She created and sold new pictures and produced work on

5.7 *Shooting the Rapids*, **by Frances Anne Hopkins. While many artists could only portray rapids as a formless froth of water, Frances was able to accurately convey the colour and texture of turbulent water as it swirled over and around the rocks.**

commission. At one point she gave financial assistance to her son Raymond, probably using money she had earned as an artist.

When Frances died at age eighty-three, she was far from famous. Her images of fur trade life, which still appear on posters, stamps, brochures and as illustrations in history books, are familiar to many Canadians. They have often been reproduced without credit however, so today the name Frances Anne Hopkins is almost unknown. Little attention was paid to Frances in Canada or anywhere else until 1990, when the Thunder Bay Art Gallery organized the first major exhibition of her works.

A talented but neglected artist, Frances Anne Hopkins captured on canvas a vanished way of life that Canada will never see again.

Further suggested reading:

Clark, Janet E. and Robert Stacey. *Frances Anne Hopkins 1838-1919: Canadian Scenery*, 1990, Thunder Bay Art Gallery, Thunder Bay (art exhibit catalogue)

Harper, Russell J. *Painting in Canada*. Toronto: University of Toronto Press, 1966.

SYLVIA ESTES STARK
—————— (1839 - 1944) ——————

I see the hand of God, guiding me through all my troubles, guiding me to the higher life.

— Sylvia Estes Stark

Sylvia stood on the shore of Saltspring Island gazing at its beauty. Her two children laughed and splashed along the edge of the Pacific Ocean, then chased each other around the family possessions that sat in small piles along the shoreline.

Her husband Louis would soon return to the beach and take them to their new home. "This island will be a fine place to raise a family," Sylvia thought with pleasure.

Suddenly seven large Haida canoes, loaded with furs, appeared in the bay. Sylvia's Cowichan guides stiffened as the canoes turned sharply and headed toward the tiny group on the seashore.

"They must be an enemy nation," Sylvia thought as she pulled her children close to her. "Please God, do not let them kill my children," she prayed frantically. "Let them be safe. And what would happen to my children if anything happened to me."

She had survived slavery. She had survived the white nightriders. She had survived the terrible overland trip to California. Was her life now going to end on a beach off the Pacific coast?

BORN A SLAVE

Sylvia Estes was born in 1839 in the slave state of Missouri. Sylvia was a slave, as were her parents, Howard and Hannah Estes.

Until 1865, when the Thirteenth Amendment to the Constitution of the United States outlawed slavery, most American blacks were slaves and lived on plantations where there were fifty to a hundred other slaves. Slave owners could be kind or cruel, and there were no laws to protect slaves from cruel masters. Whippings and other harsh punishments could be inflicted at any time at the whim of the master. Slaves with kind masters worried that they or their family members would someday be sold to someone who was cruel. Usually slaves worked from sunrise to sunset, six days a week. Even children were put to work. Sylvia was often bullied by her owner's wife. She recalled that at the age of nine she was forced to look after one of her master's children, even though Sylvia herself was sick with fever.

It was even illegal in Missouri for a slave to learn to read. Sylvia learned nonetheless by paying attention when her master's children did their lessons.

Sylvia's father, a cowboy, was owned by a Scotsman named Tom Estes. Sylvia, her brother and sister and her mother rarely saw him, as they were owned by a German baker named Charles Leopold. Howard Estes decided, however, that he and his family must be free.

FREEDOM

When Sylvia was nine years old, gold was discovered in California. Soon people were flocking to the territory by the thousands, and the price of every sort of commodity skyrocketed. Seeing his opportunity, Howard's owner sent his sons and Howard on a cattle drive to California. Howard asked for and received permission from his owner to work in California until he earned enough money to buy his own freedom and that of his wife and children. Tom Estes promised to sell Howard his freedom for $1000.

Howard worked in the California gold fields and, in time, sent $1000 back to his owner and $1000 to his wife's owner. Howard's owner, however, went back on his word, kept the money for himself, and refused to consider the $1000 as purchase money.

Sylvia's master, Charles Leopold, was a more honourable man, and he even launched a court case on Howard's behalf. The court finally decided that Howard Estes had the right to buy his freedom. By that time, however, most of the money Howard had sent had been used up by the court case. However, he continued to work in California until he again had enough money to buy his family's freedom and his own.

NIGHTRIDERS

Once they had their freedom, Howard and Hannah bought a forty-acre farm in Clay County, Missouri. The farm prospered, but they did not stay long. A band of armed white nightriders began harassing free black farmers, threatening them with death if they stayed in the area. In face of this organized terror, the Estes family decided to find a safer place to live. About the same time, Charles Leopold, Hannah Estes' former owner, decided to move cattle and sheep across the continent to California. He hired Howard as a cowboy and Hannah as a cook.

In April of 1851, the Estes started on the long Overland Trek that began in Missouri and ended almost six months later in California. Twelve-year-old Sylvia never forgot the hazardous, 4000-kilometre journey.

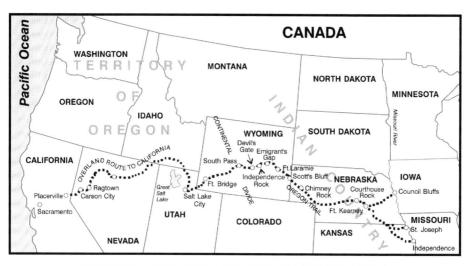

OVERLAND TRAIL TO CALIFORNIA

WESTWARD HO!

Sylvia and her family took part in one of the largest migrations in modern American history. Between 1840 and 1870, a quarter of a million people pushed through "Indian Country" west of the wide Missouri River and headed for the Territories of Oregon and California.

Some went west to claim cheap farmland in the territories. Others went hoping to strike it rich in the gold fields of California. The Estes family went hoping to find a place where they could enjoy their new freedom and live in peace. They were prepared to travel a trail that wound across what is now Kansas, Nebraska, Wyoming, Utah, Idaho and Nevada, in order to start a new life in California, where slavery was illegal.

LIFE ON THE OVERLAND TRAIL

The trip was a gruelling one, but by the 1850s many young families were heading west by wagon train. It is estimated that one out of every five of the Overland women was in some stage of pregnancy during the trip.

As they travelled along, the Overland women looked after their children and tended to the domestic chores of cooking, washing, mending, milking the cows and caring for the sick. The canvas-covered wagons heated up to over 40°C by noon. In order to lighten the load, women and children often walked behind the wagons in the choking clouds of dust.

In addition, the women drove ox teams, fetched water, and gathered wood and buffalo droppings (nicknamed "buffalo chips") and weeds to fuel the cooking fires. They also searched for wild berries, roots and herbs to give variety to an otherwise dull diet of beans, bread and coffee. Since they had not brought tables, they prepared the food on the ground. One Overlander noted that when mosquitoes got into the bread dough, the dough turned black.

The women and the children of Sylvia's age were also responsible for unpacking the tents and the bedding every night and packing them back up into the wagon every morning.

Crossing the prairies, Sylvia watched in awe as herds of buffalo stampeded ahead of the wagons. One night an arrow was shot into the camp and the next day the party was pursued by First Nations horsemen who whooped and shouted as they rode. It was a custom among First Nations to offer tribute gifts whenever they entered another nation's territory. Wagons that insolently crossed a nation's territory without payment were therefore considered to be intruders. Sylvia's frightened group gave horses, flour and other provisions to their pursuers, who were satisfied with these tribute gifts and left.

Sometimes the First Nations were helpful guides along the trail. Other times, they traded dried buffalo meat and salmon to hungry Overland families whose men were good farmers but poor hunters. The women who travelled the Overland Trail quickly realized the real enemies of the wagon train were accident and disease.

ENEMIES OF THE ROAD

Life on the trail was hazardous for children like Sylvia. Some fell out of the wagons and were crushed to death, and some were killed in cattle stampedes; some drowned as they crossed rivers, and some were lost among the hundreds of other wagons heading west at the same time.

As the springless wagons bumped along the trail, women tended the sick and the dying. Typhoid, mountain fever, dysentery and measles claimed their victims, but the greatest killer of all was cholera. It followed the wagon trains west and grew into an epidemic. Some wagon trains lost three quarters of their members; sometimes entire families died of the disease. Graves lined the sides of the westward trail, and during the height of the cholera epidemic travellers noted that gravediggers were rarely out of sight.

Lack of fresh water along the trail for humans and for the herds of cattle, sheep and horses was another concern. They often found the creeks were full of cattle carcasses that had polluted the water.

Sylvia's family finally arrived in California in September of 1851. The trip had been a grueling one, which only the tough, and the lucky, survived. Sylvia never forgot the pregnant ewes that could not keep up with the rest of the stock and were abandoned to the wolves along the trail.

GOODBYE CALIFORNIA

The Estes family settled near the mining town of Placerville, where they grew vegetables and fruit and Sylvia's mother washed clothes for the miners. The

6.1 Black Pioneers: Mildred Lewis Ware, two of her children and her husband John. The Wares were an early black family in Alberta and owned a ranch near Calgary.

family prospered, but the peace they were seeking was not so easily found. Anti-black feeling was strong in the West. In the 1850s the California legislature passed laws that said blacks could not give evidence in court against whites; blacks had to be registered to work; black children could not attend state schools. Attempts were also made to limit further black immigration. As well, California turned out to be a violent place where gunfire settled many disputes. As a small minority group, blacks could not feel safe.

In the late 1850s many members of the California black community decided it was time to leave. They had experienced slavery in the American slave states and they had experienced legalized injustice in the supposedly "free" state of California. As a result they did not want to live in the United States, or in any territory that might become part of the United States.

In 1858, the leader of the black community received a letter from Governor James Douglas of Vancouver Island, a British colony to the north. Governor Douglas's letter from Victoria encouraged them to immigrate to the British Northwest. The black community quickly sent an advance party, which returned with glowing reports about the colony. That year between six and eight hundred blacks left California to start a new life in what is today the province of British Columbia.

IDEAL IMMIGRANTS

The Oregon Treaty of 1846 set the boundary between British and American territory along the Pacific Ocean at the 49th parallel. Governor James Douglas, however, realized that with relatively few British subjects living north of that line, there was little to stop an American takeover of the entire Northwest. When rumours of gold along the Fraser River reached California in 1858, many Americans rushed to the new gold fields in British territory. The sudden influx alarmed Governor Douglas. "If the majority of immigrants be American," he wrote, "there will always be a hankering in their minds after annexation to the United States."

The California blacks were often skilled and educated, and because of American slavery, they could be counted on to resist an American takeover of the British colony. As well, Victoria suffered from a labour shortage, and this new group of industrious workers would have no trouble finding employment. It was, therefore, a shrewd move on the part of Governor Douglas to invite the California blacks to live in British North America.

Many blacks settled in Victoria or in other locations on Vancouver Island. Some were attracted by nearby Saltspring Island, and others decided to try their luck in the mainland gold fields.

A NEW HOME

In 1855, Sylvia had married a handsome, but bad-tempered dairy farmer named Louis Stark, the son of a female slave and her white owner. By 1860, when both the Estes and Stark families decided to emigrate to the British Northwest, Sylvia had given birth to two children and was pregnant with a third.

Sylvia's parents bought a farm in Saanich, near Victoria, on Vancouver Island, while Sylvia and her husband chose to settle on nearby Saltspring Island. Saltspring was mountainous but had many areas suitable for farming, and the climate was moderate. There was game on the island, mussels and clams along the seashore, and excellent fishing.

The land was rich, but there were also problems on Saltpring Island that would plague Sylvia and her family for years. The wolves, bears and cougars on the island attacked their livestock. The island could only be reached by dangerous canoe trips or by steamer. The Cowichans, one of the First Nations who lived on Vancouver Island and other nearby islands, considered Saltspring part of their territory. They traditionally made trips to the island every year and did not welcome the invasion of their land by outsiders. There were also a number of clashes in the 1860s between the Cowichans and the northern First Nations who travelled to Victoria every summer. The settlers were frightened by these battles and by the possibility of being swept into the fighting.

The first few hours Sylvia spent on Saltspring Island were frightening ones. She was terrified when some Haida warriors came ashore and examined her family's possessions piled up on the beach. The Haida leader even brandished a knife, and Sylvia was greatly relieved when instead of killing her and her two small children, he offered his companions' help to carry her goods to her home. When it was explained that her husband was coming back with help, the Haida returned to their canoes and left.

6.2 Black Pioneers of British Columbia: Nancy and Charles Alexander

After this first ordeal, Sylvia faced a second one when she viewed her new house for the first time. Louis Stark had come ahead to the island, to get things ready for his family. However, he had spent much of his time and energy clearing the land, rather than building a house. The rough cabin that was to be their home did not even have a door or a roof! Feeling lonely and depressed, still shaken by the incident on the beach, Sylvia sat down and cried. Willis, her three-year-old son, tried to cheer her up. Sylvia had endured many hardships, however, and she was strong and resilient. She hung a quilt in the doorway and neighbours soon helped to put a roof on the house.

6.3 Black Pioneers of British Columbia: Josephine Sullivan

6.4 Black Pioneers of British Columbia: Mary Lowe Barnsworth

LIFE ON SALTSPRING ISLAND

Sylvia and her husband lived as pioneers on Saltspring Island for fifteen years. They pulled out tree stumps with oxen, planted fruit trees and grew vegetables and wheat. They raised cattle, chickens, turkeys and pigs. The turkeys eventually went wild and sometimes bears attacked the pigs, but the Starks persevered. Sylvia, often left alone for days or weeks when Louis went to Victoria for provisions, became devoutly religious and believed her life was guided by a higher power.

American, English and German settlers also lived on the farms that were scattered across Saltspring Island. Sylvia sometimes helped the other islanders by working, without pay, as a nurse and midwife.

Winter was usually mild on Saltspring. During the winter of 1861-62, however, it became so cold that over a hundred head of cattle starved to death on the island. In March of 1862, a white man who was sick with smallpox arrived in Victoria from San Francisco. The disease quickly reached epidemic proportions in the coastal villages of the First Nations, where the population was already weakened by the hard winter. It is estimated that at least twenty thousand members of the First Nations died during the smallpox epidemic that began in 1862.

TROUBLES

Sylvia and her family were quickly vaccinated against the terrible disease, but the vaccination made Louis ill. He became so delirious with fever that Sylvia was afraid to leave him while she fetched the doctor. In spite of her nursing skills, she could not reduce the dreadful swelling in the vaccinated arm. As she nursed Louis she also milked their fourteen cows, fed the chickens and pigs and carried on with the usual household chores of a pioneer woman. When Louis was no longer delirious, Sylvia made the long walk to the doctor's and brought him back to their farm. Louis eventually recovered and regained the use of his arm.

Relations with the Cowichans, who resented the intruders on their land, were strained. Pioneers were occasionally threatened, shot at and even murdered. On one occasion five Cowichans wandered into the Stark cabin and began to examine its contents. During a scuffle over Louis's loaded rifle, a bullet tore through the roof when the gun went off, and the intruders quickly left.

By 1869, a number of settlers had been murdered and the Starks found it hard to hire field hands to work on their remote farm. Sylvia and Louis, who now had six children, moved to a less isolated farm on the island in an area called Fruitville.

CHANGES

Most of the black population eventually left Saltspring Island for economic reasons. The children and grandchildren of the black pioneers moved mainly to Vancouver, Victoria or, after the abolition of slavery, to the United States. In 1875, Sylvia and most of the family (Willis stayed on to farm their Saltspring property) moved to an area near Nanaimo on Vancouver Island. Here, Sylvia gave birth to her seventh child.

Although the black community in British Columbia was not barred from churches or common schools, there were occasions when they were discriminated against in places of entertainment or in restaurants. For the most part, however, the black population of British Columbia experienced a greater amount of equality than could be found anywhere else in Canada or the United States.

Sylvia, however, was unhappy on Vancouver Island. She missed the Fruitville farm and her friends and neighbours there. Moody, quarrelsome Louis was often away prospecting for gold, and when he was around, he and Sylvia frequently fought. At the age of forty-six, Sylvia left Louis and returned to the farm on Saltspring Island, which she ran with her son Willis. Louis later died near Nanaimo, possibly murdered in a quarrel over mineral rights.

For the rest of her life, Sylvia and Willis worked their Saltspring farm. Even at the age of 100, Sylvia cleared and planted her own garden.

Sylvia Estes Stark, the respected and hard-working woman who began life as a slave, died at the age of 105.

Further suggested reading:

Gould, Jan. *The Women of British Columbia.* Saanichton, British Columbia: Hancock House Publishers Ltd., 1975.

Killian, Crawford. *Go Do Some Great Thing: The Black Pioneers of British Columbia.* Vancouver: Douglas & McIntyre, 1978.

Scott, Victoria and Ernest Jones. *Sylvia Stark, a pioneer.* Seattle: Open Hand Publishing Inc., 1991.

CHAPTER 7

EDUCATOR

ADELAIDE HUNTER HOODLESS

(1857 - 1910)

Educate a boy and you educate a man, but educate a girl and you educate a family.

— Adelaide Hunter Hoodless

"Why did my baby die, Doctor?" Adelaide asked. When her son had suddenly sickened and died, Adelaide Hoodless had thought her heart would break. But now she was beyond tears. Now she wanted answers.

The doctor sighed, for he had seen many cases like this. "It was the cow's milk," he gently replied.

"The milk!" Adelaide was shocked.

"Yes. Your son got sick because he drank contaminated milk. Have you ever noticed how the flies swarm over the open cans when the milk is delivered to your home?" Adelaide nodded and the doctor continued. "Well flies carry disease, and they pass it on to the milk."

Adelaide's shock turned to horror. "But I had no idea milk could be contaminated that way. Are you ... are you saying my baby's death could have been prevented?"

The doctor nodded wearily.

Adelaide's horror turned to anger. "Then why doesn't somebody teach women about the dangers of contaminated milk?" she demanded. "Why?"

EARLY LIFE

Adelaide Hunter was born on 27 February 1857, on a farm near the village of St. George, Ontario. She was the youngest of twelve children, and her father died several months before she was born. Growing up in a large, hardworking farm family, Adelaide gained first-hand knowledge of the problems that country women faced.

At the age of twenty-four, Adelaide married John Hoodless, who was a partner in a thriving furniture company in Hamilton, Ontario. For eight years, Adelaide lived a happy, busy life with her prosperous husband and their four young children. Then tragedy struck. Her youngest son, John Harold, died when he was only one and a half years old. At that time, it was not unusual for children to die. In fact, one out of every five died before reaching adulthood, and every cemetery contained many small graves.

Adelaide, however, refused to accept her baby's death as simply "God's will." She set out to find the cause of her son's death, but when she did, she was haunted by her discovery.

THE TERRIBLE "GOOD OLD DAYS"

The conditions in homes in the 1800s would shock most of us today. Houses were lit by candles or coal oil lamps with glass chimneys. The burning coal oil, or kerosene, gave off a black smoke that coated the glass chimneys and everything else it touched, including the walls, with greasy soot.

Before the invention of screens, flies and other insects swarmed into houses, especially the kitchens, through open doors and windows. There were no refrigerators, and ice boxes were neither common nor efficient. Houses did not have running water, let alone toilets, and open wells, which were easily polluted, could cause epidemics of diseases such as typhoid fever.

Horse-drawn dairy wagons plodded up and down the dusty streets carrying large, open cans of milk for home delivery. Such milk was a dangerous substance for many customers. Unscrupulous dairies sometimes added water, chalk and other ingredients in order to stretch the milk supply. This could lead to problems known as "milk poison," "the trembles" or "milk evil." Some dairies used the milk of diseased cows.

7.1 Adelaide believed "A nation cannot rise above the level of its homes; therefore women must work and study together to raise our homes to the highest possible level."

Cows that were sick with tuberculosis (a lung disease also called consumption) passed the disease on to the humans who drank their milk. Even dairies that did not cheat the customer or use diseased cows paid little attention to the flies that clustered around the open cans of milk in the heat of summer.

Milk is nutritious for humans and germs alike, and in such conditions it often became infected and caused a sickness known as the "summer complaint." Many children died of the summer complaint, including, in 1889, Adelaide's baby son.

Louis Pasteur, a French chemist, had discovered in the 1860s that heating milk for thirty minutes at 63°C and then rapidly cooling it destroyed the disease-producing germs in milk. This process, known as pasteurization, was not immediately adopted in Canada, and many Canadians in the late 1800s continued to sicken and die from drinking contaminated milk.

IGNORANCE IS DANGEROUS

Adelaide was tormented by the knowledge that her baby son had died from contaminated milk. It was a senseless death that she could have prevented if she had been properly warned. She wondered why the public schools did not teach female students the type of information that would one day save the lives of their own families. The government made no attempt to teach women how to care for their children and run their households. How, then, in a rapidly changing world, could women find out about new scientific discoveries and put them to use in their own homes?

Adelaide could have spent the rest of her life wrapped in a shell of bitterness, continually blaming herself or others for the death of her son. Instead, she decided to dedicate the rest of her life to teaching girls and women the complicated science of child care and home management. For ignorance of sanitation and nutrition, as she knew from her own sad experience, could be deadly.

EDUCATION

Adelaide made herself an authority on household management by reading everything she could find on the topics of domestic science (also known as home economics) and the teaching of domestic science. She obtained information from European countries on their programs and visited domestic science schools in the United States to study their methods.

When a Young Women's Christian Association (YWCA) was organized in the city of Hamilton in late 1889, Adelaide realized that this was her chance to begin teaching women about home nutrition and sanitation. The YWCA began to give cooking classes, and Adelaide

7.2 Women's unpaid work: Ottawa, 1892. Most women spent the day after wash day ironing clothes. A number of heavy irons were heated on the stove. When one iron cooled, the woman replaced it on the stove and took a hot iron fresh from the fire.

persuaded the Hamilton School Board to send female students to attend them. The classes were an immediate success.

THE CULT OF MOTHERHOOD

The "work" produced by the family changed dramatically in the 1800s. Before the Industrial Revolution, men, women and children had often worked together in the home, growing or producing by hand items that the family could use or sell at market. Once machinery was invented to mass produce items, however, people were expected to work at the place where the machinery was located. More and more husbands and even children began to go off every morning to work for wages in factories and offices.

Suddenly the home was no longer viewed as a place of work. Mothers, who were generally left behind at the home in order to care for small children and carry out the unpaid household chores, now felt isolated and invisible as the only adults in the house. As well, they often felt that their work was not valued by society; unlike other workers, they could not contribute a pay cheque to the family unit. Some women at home began to feel they were not valued as "workers" and that their type of work was no longer important to society.

By the 1850s, however, the rapid growth of cities was raising concern about street crime and young criminals. The home began to be viewed as the place where children were shaped, like a piece of clay, for good or for bad. As fathers were now assumed to be away from home earning wages, mothers were now expected to make sure that their children's minds, souls and bodies were properly enriched.

These beliefs, which some historians today refer to as the "cult of motherhood," raised the role of mothering to great heights. Churches, "experts" and even the popular music of the time bombarded women with the message that all mothers were tender, kind, innocent, pure and selfless.

It was not clearly explained why or how the half of the population that was female would suddenly turn into long-suffering saints the moment they gave birth to a child. Nevertheless, the cult of motherhood insisted that mothers were morally superior creatures, were important, and could now be held completely responsible for the behaviour of their children. If women could not feel valued as paid workers, now they could at least feel that society admired them for being mothers. Today, some historians suggest that the cult of motherhood was promoted to distract women from the fact that married females in the 1800s had almost no legal rights and almost no financial power.

Society's admiration for motherhood was not without its price. People began to blame the mother, and only the mother, for each and every shortcoming or failure of even her adult children. As well, many mothers felt that no matter how they tried, they could not provide for all the moral, physical and spiritual needs of their children. Motherhood and guilt were now entwined.

WOMEN WORKING TOGETHER

Women who felt isolated in their homes began to band together in women's organizations. They wanted to overcome loneliness and find solutions to common problems. Women's organizations often demanded greater recognition for women and greater respect for the unpaid labour of women. It was not merely household work, women's groups argued, it was domestic science.

In 1893, Adelaide, who was now the president of the Hamilton YWCA, attended a Women's Congress in Chicago, Illinois. There she met representatives of women's groups from all over the world. Meeting and

7.3 Domestic Science in the home: Toronto, early 1900s

7.4 Domestic Science in the home: Saskatchewan, 1906

sharing experiences with all these other groups made Adelaide and other Canadian women at the meeting realize that they could accomplish much more by working together on a national level. Because the cult of motherhood insisted women were morally superior, many women of that period came to believe the role of mother gave women invaluable wisdom and insight that they could use to improve not just their own families, but all of society. When Adelaide returned home, she began a letter-writing campaign that resulted in local YWCAs drawing together to create the national YWCA of Canada. That year, Lady Aberdeen, wife of the new Governor General of Canada and a great believer in the importance and power of women's groups, launched the National Council of Women of Canada (NCWC) with Adelaide as its treasurer.

Education is the responsibility of the provincial governments, and at the National Council of Women's first annual meeting in 1894, Adelaide took on the task of encouraging all provincial governments to give domestic science training to Canadian school girls. At a time when women rarely spoke in public, Adelaide gave over sixty speeches between 1894 and 1896 to teachers' conventions and school boards, emphasizing the importance of domestic science education.

As a result of the efforts of Adelaide and the National Council of Women, provinces including Ontario, New Brunswick, Nova Scotia, Manitoba and British Columbia soon established domestic science courses in the public schools.

THE BIRTH OF THE WOMEN'S INSTITUTE

In February 1897, Adelaide spoke to a Ladies Night meeting of the Farmers' Institute. "You are in the midst of a campaign to improve the health of your animals," she told the male farmers. "I am here to tell you the health of your wives and children is more important." Then, possibly remembering the difficulties her own mother had faced as a farm wife, Adelaide suggested that rural women should have an institute of their own.

The words of this wealthy city woman irritated some of the men, but a number of the women were impressed. The chairman quickly arranged a special meeting for the following Friday evening and asked Adelaide to speak again. One hundred and one women showed up in Stoney Creek, Ontario, on February 19 to discuss the formation of an institute for women.

Adelaide firmly believed in the importance and responsibilities of motherhood and suggested that the well-being of society depended on what happened inside the home. The home, she insisted, was more important than the world of men. If rural men needed an organization that helped them become better farmers, she argued, then rural women needed a similar organization to help them with their important work.

The women were convinced, and less than a week later the first regular meeting of the new Women's Institute was held in a home in Winona, near Hamilton. Adelaide Hoodless became honorary president. The Institute's objective was to promote the knowledge of domestic science, including household sanitation, household design, nutrition and "a more scientific care of children."

Originally the Women's Institute had started out as part of the Farmer's Institute. Soon, however, the women decided to declare their independence. The Farmers' Institute fought against this break, and its superintendent confidently declared, "If the ladies of the province strike out on independent lines, it will be a long time before they receive recognition." He was wrong.

THE POWER OF AN IDEA

Rural women of the 1800s faced a degree of isolation we find hard to imagine today. Unlike city women, they felt cut off from much of the

7.5 An Alberta woman churns butter, 1908. Rural women felt cut off from much of the world.

world. Radio, movies and television, the inventions that bring entertainment, current events and education into today's homes, did not yet exist. Few rural areas could boast a lending library, and the biggest social event of the year was often the school Christmas concert. Yet rural women were just as concerned as city women were about the welfare of their families and their communities.

It is no wonder, then, that Women's Institutes spread like wildfire. Within four months of that first meeting in Stoney Creek, two more Institutes had been formed. By 1902 there were twenty-four, by 1904 there were 149, and by 1907 there were 500 Women's Institutes. Adelaide's idea of a practical, educational self-help association for rural women would eventually grow into a coast-to-coast Canadian organization with thousands of branches and tens of thousands of members.

ACCOMPLISHMENTS

The Women's Institute became a type of rural university for women and was the beginning of the adult education movement. Provincial governments began to send lecturers to the groups to discuss practical subjects such as cooking, dressmaking and, because doctors were often far away, home nursing.

The women learned, and they also worked together to enrich rural life. In many communities the local Women's Institute introduced dental clinics into the schools as well as a hot lunch program and music as a subject. Some Institutes provided playground equipment and swimming pools, helped set up libraries, encouraged amateur singing and drama, and lobbied for the pasteurization of milk. The Women's Institute motto "For Home and Country," adopted at the suggestion of Adelaide Hoodless, was familiar to many grateful communities.

CANADA'S GREATEST EXPORT

The Women's Institute, begun so modestly by Adelaide Hoodless, spread to Great Britain and then into over a hundred countries around the world. The organization encouraged rural women of all races, colours and creeds to help themselves.

In 1933 an international organization for Women's Institutes and other similar organizations of rural women was set up under the name of the Associated Country Women of the World. It has been said that the Women's Institute is Canada's greatest export.

UNDER ATTACK

Both the National Council of Women and the Women's Institute gave the women of Canada a place where they could share and exchange knowledge, opinions and beliefs. At a time when women were rarely expected to venture from the home except to do church work, large, visible women's organizations were sometimes criticized. When it was decided that the meetings of the National Council of Women would start with silent prayer in order to avoid offending women from different religious backgrounds, the headline of an Ottawa newspaper unfairly shrieked "NCW Against Lord's Prayer."

Even Adelaide Hoodless, who lived in a time when all women were expected to be homemakers and who devoted her life to the good of the Canadian home and family, received bitter criticism. Some felt that teaching domestic science was a "fool fad" that would increase school expenses. Others could not understand why an attractive, well-to-do married woman would want to travel and lecture across the country.

There were also those who wished to cling to their ignorance, for the view that all childhood death was the unavoidable will of God, released parents from responsibility. These people resisted Adelaide's message that home sanitation could save lives. Instead, they criticized the messenger. In spite of Adelaide's hard work and many contributions to family life in Canada, they sourly commented, "Let her stay home and take care of her own family."

Adelaide's family, however, adored her and was proud of her many accomplishments. As a lecturer on the topic of domestic science, Adelaide was one of the first women employed by the government of Ontario. She promoted the Victorian Order of Nurses, founded in 1897 by Lady Aberdeen to provide nursing care to isolated communities. Adelaide wrote a textbook on domestic science that was published in 1898, and in 1899 she was presented to Queen Victoria at the International Congress of Women in London, England.

Adelaide's daughter described her mother as someone who had "a stimulating and lovable personality that drew young and old alike. Yet," her daughter continued, "she seemed to have time for everything."

FUND RAISING TO THE END

With the Women's Institute in the hands of other capable women, Adelaide continued with her original goal of educating girls and women in the field of domestic science.

"Women must learn not to waste time on non-essentials" was one of Adelaide's sayings. Her daughter believed that much of her mother's success was due to "her wise choice of essentials," and Adelaide knew that fundraising was an essential part of her original goal.

Once schools in Canada began to offer domestic science as a course of study, there was a sudden need for domestic science teachers. Adelaide convinced the premier of Ontario that it was important to establish a school to train Canadian women to teach domestic science. It was agreed that if Adelaide could provide the building, the Ontario government would pay for its maintenance.

Adelaide immediately arranged a luncheon meeting with Montreal millionaire Sir William Macdonald. The meeting was a success and Sir William donated money to build the Macdonald Institute in Guelph, Ontario, in 1903 and Macdonald College in Quebec a few years later.

A WOMAN OF ACTION

One evening in 1910, Adelaide was fundraising in Massey Hall, Toronto, where she was speaking to a meeting of the Federation of Women's Clubs. In spite of a severe headache, she was delivering an excellent speech that would later result in the founding of the Lillian Massey School of Household Science in Toronto. Part way through her speech, the audience began to applaud and, with a smile, Adelaide paused, then collapsed and died. It was the day before her fifty-second birthday.

Adelaide Hunter Hoodless was a woman of action who transformed her own personal tragedy into a lifetime mission to prevent similar tragedies. Today, she is remembered as a woman of exceptional talent who founded or helped to found the National YWCA, the Macdonald Institute, the National Council of Women of Canada, the Victorian Order of Nurses and the Women's Institute. The home where she was born is owned by the Federated Women's Institutes of Canada and is a museum known as the Adelaide Hunter Hoodless Homestead.

Further suggested reading:

Howes, Ruth. "Adelaide Hunter Hoodless." In Mary Quayle Innis, ed. *The Clear Spirit*. Toronto: University of Toronto Press, 1966.

Norcross, E. Blanche. *Pioneers Every One*. Toronto: Burns & MacEachern Limited, 1979.

CHAPTER 8

WITNESS TO THE BUFFALO DAYS

VICTORIA BELCOURT CALLIHOO

(1861 - 1966)

When the herd was started it was just a dark solid moving mass. We, of those days, never could believe the buffalo would ever be killed off, for there were thousands and thousands.

— Victoria Callihoo

Silently the boy handed his mother the loaded gun. Victoria had sent her son running back for her old muzzle-loader while she watched the bear move about the woods. Now the tall, dark-haired woman lifted her gun and took careful aim; if she only wounded the huge animal, it might attack. Keeping her body perfectly still, Victoria fired. There was a roar from the muzzle-loader and the bear dropped dead.

Victoria turned to her son with a smile. "We can put this bear to good use," she said with satisfaction.

MÉTIS HERITAGE

Victoria Belcourt was born on 19 November 1861, in the Métis community of Lac Ste Anne, in what is now the province of Alberta. She was named after Queen Victoria, the Queen of England.

At the time of Victoria's birth, Lac Ste Anne, which is located northwest of Edmonton, was part of Rupert's Land, the vast territory that drained into Hudson Bay and that was owned and controlled by the Hudson's Bay Company. The area would not become a part of Canada for another eight years.

Victoria's father was Métis, one of a people formed as a result of three centuries of intermarriage between French men and First Nations women. The word Métis comes from an old French word for mixed. The children of the mixed marriages were called Métis and they often married other children of mixed marriages; their children were also called Métis. The children of marriages between Scottish or English men and First Nations women, however, were often referred to as mixed bloods.

8.1 A Métis family

The early European trader discovered that marriage to a First Nations woman gave him status among the First Nations that he would not otherwise have. Understandably, the First Nations trusted relatives more than strangers, and the European trader became a relative by marriage to one of their women. Marriage gave the trader a network of helpers and trading partners among his wife's relatives. A talented, hard-working First Nations wife also transformed animal skins into clothing and shelter, and acted as interpreter and guide in the wilderness. For her part, marriage to a European man gave a First Nations woman and her relatives access to the useful European trade network.

The Métis people adopted elements from both the French and the First Nations, and gradually formed a distinct and unique cultural group.

8.2 Laetitia Bird, a "mixed blood"

8.3 First Women: Cree

MEDICINE WOMAN

Victoria's Cree mother was a highly respected medicine woman. There were no drug stores, so medicine women spent much of their time gathering the inner bark of yellow willow, leaves and flowers of cowslips, chokecherry bark, bluebell roots, rose hips and cow parsnips that they needed for their medicines. They also used ingredients such as slippery elm bark, lily of the valley flowers, mint leaf and the roots and stems of burdock.

Many of the collected plants were carefully dried, reduced to a powder, and then stored in leather pouches or birchbark containers that were identified by coded marks. Some were taken internally in the form of herbal teas, or in the form of vapours that were inhaled when powdered herbs were sprinkled on hot stones. Some remedies were applied externally in the form of poultices, salves or ointments.

The healers of the First Nations had remedies for ailments ranging from poison ivy and snake or insect bites to headaches, swelling caused by sprains or other injuries, diarrhea, constipation, external infection, external ulcers and bleeding. They also treated coughs, colds, sore throats, rheumatism, frostbite, fever, earaches, indigestion, boils, nervousness, stomach ache, blood poisoning and burns. Some healers even amputated limbs that were dangerously infected.

Victoria later recalled that her mother's healing skills were in great demand during the exciting but dangerous buffalo hunts that the Métis held twice a year.

8.4 First Women: Blackfoot

8.5 First Women: Blood

IN SEARCH OF BUFFALO

Victoria was thirteen when she went on her first of four buffalo hunts. The hunt was an important part of Métis life, for the Métis relied on the buffalo for much of their livelihood. Not only did the buffalo provide food and shelter for the Métis themselves, but the nourishing buffalo meat product known as pemmican was a valuable trade item.

For the spring hunt, the Métis of Lac Ste Anne left as soon as their small fields were planted and headed south to find the buffalo herds on the prairies. Every year the buffalo moved back and forth along the same route between their summer and winter ranges.

As Victoria's family and others from the area travelled toward the buffalo migration route, more and more Métis would join their group until there were about a hundred families in the hunt. Métis scouts were sent ahead to make sure the group did not run into Blackfoot warriors. The Blackfoot nation was the traditional enemy of both the Métis and the Cree, and it was safer for Métis to travel and hunt in large groups.

The rivers and streams could be dangerously high with spring floods, but there were no bridges and the waters had to be crossed with care. When the water was deep, the horses would swim and the wooden Red River carts of the Métis would be floated across. Victoria's family usually took three Red River carts on the hunt to haul the buffalo meat back to Lac Ste Anne.

On Victoria's first hunt, the Métis found the huge buffalo herd one day's travel south of the North Saskatchewan River. On later trips, however, they had to travel farther and farther south as the herds began to disappear.

SETTING UP CAMP

Like the First Nations of the plains, the Métis lived in tipis while travelling and hunting. Tipis were strong, warm, waterproof and easily put up and taken down. The Métis carried the tipi poles and tipi covers with them, and set up their camps close to water. Tipi covers were originally made of buffalo skins sewn tightly together. Later, the Métis used canvas cloth, which was lighter in weight and could be obtained from European traders.

The tipis were set up in a large circle, which enclosed a smaller, tighter circle of carts. At night, the fastest horses were kept safe inside the enclosure formed by the carts. The most prized possession of a Métis hunter was a fast horse; a fast horse meant more buffalo could be killed. The rest of the horses were herded together and also carefully guarded as horse stealing was common on the prairies.

AFTER THE HUNT

Many Cree and Blackfoot still hunted buffalo with the traditional bow and arrow. The Métis hunters, however, shot the animals with muzzle-loaders and single-barrel flint-locks. Some of them could reload as they galloped along with the herd, while others wheeled off, reloaded their guns and then rode back into the stampeding buffalo.

A chase only lasted a few noisy and confused minutes, but most Métis hunters killed at least one buffalo during that time, and some might kill as many as three. Sometimes a galloping horse would catch a hoof in a badger hole and the rider would be thrown and trampled. Sometimes a buffalo would attack and gore a horse or rider with its horns.

As a medicine woman, Victoria's mother then set to work setting broken bones and tending to the other injuries suffered during the chase. The other women came out from the camp with the Red River carts and began the hard work of skinning and butchering the buffalo carcasses.

The Métis used everything from the buffalo except the bones, horns and hoofs. Victoria and her people used the buffalo hide for ropes, robes, footwear, bags, clothes and tipi covers. Buffalo meat was cooked or dried at the hunting camp before the Métis left for home.

To dry the meat, the women placed rails between two sets of wooden tripods and then hung thin strips of buffalo meat over them. Under the rails, young women such as Victoria used pieces of flint to start small fires. They fed the fires with wood brought with them from the north and with dried buffalo droppings, which they collected on the prairies. The smoke kept the flies away from the meat and gave it a smoky flavour. The dried buffalo meat was still too bulky for Victoria's family to cart all the way back to Lac Ste Anne, so it was made into pemmican. Not only was pemmican portable and easily stored, but Victoria described it as "the best and most nourishing food I ever ate."

PEMMICAN

One of the major trade items of the late 1700s, pemmican probably originated with the First Nations of the plains. Originally, pemmican could be made with the meat from various kinds of big game animals or even with fish, but buffalo was always the favourite ingredient.

At the Métis hunting camp, the thin strips of dried buffalo meat were pounded into powder. The women then added sun-dried saskatoon berries and melted animal fat and packed the mixture into bags made of buffalo hide. The bags were then sewn shut with buffalo sinew. Pemmican packed inside the airtight skins could keep for two to three years.

When European traders discovered that a small amount of this nutritious food could keep a person alive for many days, pemmican quickly became a staple of the fur trade. Supplying trading posts and forts with pemmican was a major source of income for the Métis.

The Métis were usually back from the spring hunt by early August. In early September, after a month of haying and harvesting, they set off for the fall hunt. This time, they were hunting buffalo primarily for their own use. With winter approaching, it was important to have enough dried meat and pemmican to get them through the long, cold months ahead. After every hunt, the Red River carts were piled with heavy loads of pemmican and buffalo hides as Victoria and her family slowly made their way back home to Lac Ste Anne.

A MÉTIS HOME

Victoria, who was proud to call herself Métis, preferred to speak Cree, her mother's language, rather than French or English. At the age of seventeen she married Louis Callihoo, who had French, Cree and Iroquois ancestors, and the couple set up their own home.

The Métis adapted to the world around them and had developed their own way of living which was part First Nations and part European. Métis homes in the Lac Ste Anne area had only one storey and were made of dirt or hewn spruce logs. The holes between the logs were filled in and then the house was plastered with white clay. The floors and even the doors were also made of hewn logs placed tightly together. The slanted roof was covered in dried bark from spruce trees. Timber was easily obtained in the woods that were less than two kilometres from the settlement. The Métis bartered for their axes and other wood-working tools at the closest Hudson's Bay Company store.

Instead of glass, the wet rawhide skin of a calf, a deer or a moose calf was stretched over the window frames with wooden pegs. When it dried, the skin was tight. It was not transparent, but it did allow some daylight into the room.

There were no metal stoves, so Métis couples such as Victoria and Louis built an open fireplace, known as a "mud stove," in the corner of the room. They covered poles with a mud and hay mixture, and white clay was then spread on top to give a smooth finish. The area around the base was also plastered with clay so that a stray spark would not set the floor on fire. The mud stove gave the home both heat and light, for as Victoria later explained, in the 1870s her family did not have oil lamps and it was a few years before they started to make their own candles.

Victoria also recalled that the Métis homes did not contain tables, chairs or benches. A cloth was spread on the floor for meals. Their dishes, which were all from the Hudson's Bay store, were kept in a wooden corner cupboard. A piece of cloth hung over the front of the cupboard in place of a door. The cooking pots were made of seamless copper and also came from the Hudson's Bay store. If dented, the copper pots were easily hammered back into shape.

Victoria and her husband bartered for items from the Hudson's Bay store with furs. Money was just coming into use in the late 1870s and many found it confusing. Fur was the real currency of the land, and at a Hudson's Bay store a Métis would ask "How much fur for this item?"

Everyone slept on the floor on duck and goose feather mattresses and pillows. Buffalo robes and Hudson's Bay blankets were used for warmth. In the daytime, the bedding was folded up and placed in a corner of the room.

Métis women made soap, which Victoria referred to as "la potash," by mixing grease or fat with lye made from wood ashes. They made brooms by lashing willow branches together around a smooth, wooden handle. Moss, which they gathered and dried, was used in place of diapers. Babies were laced into holders stuffed with soft, dry moss that was thrown away when soiled. Dried moss, which Victoria described as "a household necessity," was also used to wipe freshly scrubbed floors.

It was a tradition that before a home had been occupied for two days, the owner had to invite all the neighbours to a big party. Victoria loved the "old-time" jigs and reels that the Métis danced on these occasions. In particular, Victoria never lost her love of the Red River jig; she won a dance contest at the age of 74 and could still dance the jig at the age of 103.

"FLOWER BEADWORK PEOPLE"

Métis women made most of their family's clothing, some from cloth purchased from the Hudson's Bay store. Women like Victoria also made overcoats for the men from buffalo skins and made outer leggings from Hudson's Bay blankets. The leggings were tied to a belt with a buckskin string. The men did not wear underwear or socks.

Women wore shawls instead of coats. They also wore moccasins, and leggings up to the knee made out of black velvet that they had beaded on the outer side of the leg. When they worked outside in cold weather, they wrapped their feet in flannel and their knees in flannelette. The women's embroidery work in glass beads or porcupine quills so often used flower designs that the Cree and the Dakota people called the Métis the "flower beadwork people."

BY CARIOLE AND TRAVOIS

Victoria was handy with a gun and was also an expert teamster. At one time, she and her husband used teams of horses to haul freight for the Hudson's Bay Company on the trail between Edmonton and Athabasca Landing.

When speed was needed, Victoria's family rode horseback. For fast travel in the snow, however, the family used a dog team harnessed to a small, light sleigh known as a cariole. A cariole could carry only one person or a relatively light load, but a dog team would run by day and by night.

The Métis sometimes used a travois when they travelled. The travois, copied from the people of the First Nations, consisted of two long poles that were crossed at one end and attached to a horse or dog. The other ends of the poles dragged along the ground. A wooden or net frame was placed between the poles to carry items such as bedding or food. For travel by water, the Métis used canoes.

MÉTIS REBELLION

The Métis faced new problems when the country of Canada purchased Rupert's Land from the Hudson's Bay Company in 1869. The Canadian government wanted the midwest settled and farmed as quickly as possible and did not care about, or consult with, the Métis already living in Rupert's Land. The Métis who lived in Winnipeg's Red River Settlement, in what is now the province of Manitoba, were afraid that their rights would not be respected and that they would lose their lands and their unique way of life.

After Manitoba joined Confederation in 1870, the Red River Métis found life there increasingly difficult. Some moved west to join other Métis settlements such as Lac Ste Anne. They hoped to continue their traditional way of life away from the European settlers flooding into Manitoba. For a time, this seemed possible. But the settlers kept pushing westward, and the Canadian government paid little attention to Métis requests for secure title to the lands they farmed. In 1885, some Métis, led by a man named Louis Riel, staged a rebellion. Riel had led an earlier uprising at Red River that had forced the government to accept Métis terms. This second rebellion would not have the same success. The Métis were defeated, and Louis Riel was tried and hanged for treason.

The Métis of Lac Ste Anne did not fight in the rebellion, but they agreed with Louis Riel's demand that Métis land rights be respected. With the buffalo gone, they realized that their land rights were more important than ever; now agriculture would be the key to their survival.

AFTER THE BUFFALO DAYS

As railways and European settlement pushed further west, the buffalo all but disappeared from the plains of North America. The loss of the buffalo tested the Métis' ability to adapt to a changed world.

Victoria and Louis raised chickens, black-and-white-spotted hogs and cattle on their tiny farm. Some Métis did not like the taste of beef, but with the buffalo gone, they had to get used to its flavour. Victoria and her twelve children lived on the farm, for Victoria believed that this was the best place to raise a family. To add to the family income, Louis also operated a sawmill and a hotel in Lac Ste Anne for a time.

Deer, moose and bear were still plentiful, and instead of buffalo hide, Victoria now used tanned moose hide to make coats, pants, mittens, gloves and moccasins. Besides their own livestock, the family also ate moose, deer, wild fowl and whitefish.

Victoria used thread from the Hudson's Bay store to make fish nets, and she made bark containers that were sewn together with tiny roots and sealed with hot spruce gum. These containers served as milk pails and berry baskets.

Victoria did not have wheat flour but grew barley on the Callihoo farm. An ox or horse pulled the plough and the seed was tossed on the ground. She added barley to soups and also cooked it in a frying pan to form a type of bread. Unhulled barley was fried until it was black and then used in place of coffee beans.

LATER YEARS

Victoria spent her entire life in the Métis community in the beautiful Lac Ste Anne area. Her husband died in 1926, and she lived on alone in her house until the age of 101. After World War II she recorded her early memories of Métis life, and three of her articles were published in the Alberta Historical Review. In 1949, she unveiled Canada's Historic Sites and Monuments cairn at Elk Island Park that commemorated Canadian efforts to save the prairie buffalo from extinction.

For many years Victoria remained a vital member of her community, and she enjoyed the frequent visits of her friends and family. Her New Year's Day Open House was always an important event for her many relatives and for the community. At the age of 90, Victoria bought a horse and enjoyed driving her horse and buggy around the area. She had her first physical examination when she was 99 and the doctor told her she was in good health. She was 100 years old when she first used the telephone.

Victoria died on 21 April 1966, at the age of 104. At her death, she had 241 descendants, including 165 great-grandchildren and 8 great-great-grandchildren. Always proud of her Métis heritage, Victoria lived to see her people change from the tipis and Red River carts of the buffalo days to the telephones and automobiles of the space age.

Further suggested reading:

MacEwan, Grant. ... *And Mighty Women Too*. Saskatoon: Western Producer Prairie Books, 1975.

Callihoo, Victoria. "Early life in Lac Ste Anne and St. Albert in the eighteen seventies." *Alberta Historical Review*, vol. 1, no. 3, November 1953, pp. 21-6.

Callihoo, Victoria. "Our Buffalo Hunts." *Alberta Historical Review*, vol. 8, no. 1, Winter 1960, pp. 24-5.

CHAPTER 9

PHYSICIAN AND SCIENTIST

DR. MAUDE ABBOTT
(1869 - 1940)

It is not simply as the world's authority on congenital heart disease that Maude will be best remembered, but as a living force in the medicine of her generation.

— Dr. Paul Whiteside, New England Heart Association

Maude paused in the doorway before entering the room. The pathologists of Great Britain were assembled for an important meeting in this Cambridge University hall.

"Look, there's Dr. Abbott at the front entrance," said the presiding officer of the meeting. "What extraordinary work she does!" he added, and rose to greet her.

Catching sight of her, the other British physicians in the hall began to applaud warmly as Dr. Maude Abbott joined their group.

A SAD BEGINNING

Maude was born in St. Andrews East, Quebec, on 18 March 1869. The Abbotts were a respectable and influential family, but Maude was born into a tragic situation. She and her older sister, Alice, were the only children of Frances Abbott Babin and Reverend Jeremiah Babin, an Anglican clergyman. In 1867, Reverend Babin was accused of murdering his crippled sister. He was tried and found not guilty, but he then abandoned his family before Maude was born. Seven months after giving birth to her, Maude's mother died of tuberculosis.

Maude and Alice were legally adopted by their widowed grandmother, Mrs. William Abbott, and their surname was changed to Abbott. Their grandmother, who was then sixty-two, was a wonderful and gracious woman who raised these two daughters of her daughter alone.

Maude and Alice were educated at their grandmother's home by a governess, but Maude, who was a born scholar, longed for more. She attended a Montreal private school for young ladies for one year and then won an entrance scholarship to McGill University in Montreal. McGill, which had been chartered in 1821, did not allow women to attend until 1884. When Maude entered in 1886, it was only the third year that women students had been accepted.

9.1 Maude Abbott. Maude developed such a world-wide reputation that any medical person from Canada who travelled abroad was often told "Ah, then, you must know Dr. Maude Abbott."

HIGHER EDUCATION FOR WOMEN

Should women be allowed to study at university? Some claimed that a woman's sole duty was to marry and spend her life looking after the needs of her husband and children; higher education for women was therefore unnecessary and wasted. Some insisted that women were weak and could not stand the strain of higher studies.

Others, however, pointed out that it was unrealistic to think that a woman would always have a husband who was ready, willing and able to support the family. Unmarried women and widowed or deserted women were expected to support themselves and their families; higher education for women would mean better employment opportunities for women who had to support themselves. Still others argued that higher education for women would create educated women who would be better wives and mothers. As sensible as these arguments seem, they failed to convince university authorities.

It was a practical reason that finally pushed universities to admit women students. There was a shortage of qualified male students and universities had huge expenses to meet. Simply put, women students were a new source of income.

Maude and other women students thrived at university. At McGill, women were usually educated in separate classes from the men students, but all students, male and female, wrote the same exams and were eligible for the same prizes. There were nine women in Maude's class and she became the class president.

The argument that women would collapse under the increased mental strain of higher education was quickly proved wrong; the scholastic achievement of the nine women in Maude's graduating class was impressive. McGill awarded five medals in 1890, and women won three of them. Maude, graduating with her Bachelor of Arts degree, won the Lord Stanley Gold Medal and was the class valedictorian. She later said that her four years in undergraduate studies at McGill were the happiest years of her life.

McGILL SAYS NO

While a student at McGill, Maude daringly decided she wanted to study medicine. On a visit home, she asked her grandmother if she could become a doctor. This remarkable woman replied, "Dear child, you may be anything you like." McGill University, however, did not agree. Although women were grudgingly being admitted into the general arts courses there and elsewhere, women who wished to attend medical school often faced great hostility.

9.2 Too delicate to be doctors: The World Champion Lady Bucking-Horse Rider, Winnipeg Stampede, 1913

Many people claimed that medicine was an unsuitable field for women, arguing that the study of the human body and the dissecting course would cause them to lose their "maidenly modesty." They also claimed women had weak nerves, unstable health, poor powers of endurance and could not withstand the stresses of medical life. In short, the home was the place for women; the world was the place for men.

In response, those in favour of women doctors pointed to the many women healers of the past. They also pointed out that the many women who toiled long, exhausting hours in factory sweatshops were proof enough of women's ability to endure hard physical labour. The question of female endurance, they suggested, was merely a smoke screen to keep women out of the well-paying professions.

Although Canada's educational system did not encourage young women to consider high-status, scientific careers, the second half of the nineteenth century saw more and more women demanding entrance into

9.3 Too delicate to be doctors: women graders during the construction of the Grand Trunk Pacific Railway, Alberta, 1907

9.4 Too delicate to be doctors: Women war workers operating cartridge case presses during World War I

9.5 Too delicate to be doctors: Farm work, Alberta, 1914

9.6 In 1883 two separate medical schools, the Kingston Women's Medical College and the Women's Medical College, Toronto, were established in Canada. Pictured here is the Dean with the Class in Surgery at Kingston, 1890.

medical school. Early women doctors like Emily Stowe and Jennie Trout had been forced to go to medical schools in the United States, but by 1890, women could study medicine at Trinity College in Toronto or Queen's University in Kingston, Ontario. Women could not, however, study medicine at McGill. Maude, who had graduated from McGill with a gold medal, was curtly refused admission to the McGill Medical School, because she was a woman.

Maude turned to her cousin, Senator John Abbott, who would become the prime minister of Canada the next year, for advice. He suggested: "Get the public at your back!" and she began a campaign to have medical courses for women started at McGill. She was not successful, and it would be another twenty-seven years before McGill's dinosaurs in stethoscopes admitted women into their medical school.

A FROSTY RECEPTION

Maude received word that Bishop's Medical College in Montreal would accept her in their school. Her problems, however, were not over. A medical student was required to visit hospital wards and could not graduate as a doctor without this hospital experience. The Montreal General Hospital was supposed to be open to the medical students of McGill and Bishop's with the purchase of a $25 ticket of admission. It was, however, up to the doctors who ran the hospital to decide who could or could not enter the hospital wards. Like the universities, the hospitals

9.7 In the late 1890s, most medical schools and hospitals were exclusive male clubs. The few women who ventured in were treated as outsiders. Here, the Resident Staff doctors at Toronto General Hospital strike a pose for the camera in 1895.

were male monopolies, and the doctors who controlled them worried about women doctors. The universities might reluctantly view women students as a new source of income, but male doctors viewed women doctors as a new source of competition.

Maude began her medical studies at Bishop's in 1890 and sent the money for her ticket of admission to the Montreal General Hospital. The hospital was afraid it would be "overrun" by women students from various medical schools and withheld her ticket.

Earlier on, some doctors had tried to discourage the trickle of new female doctors by threatening to resign as instructors if universities admitted women students. Now, they began to erect barriers against women doctors at every step in their medical careers. Refusing to allow women students such as Maude into hospital wards was one such barrier.

FINANCIAL FEARS

Male doctors felt that their profession was already overcrowded, but women doctors presented a special threat to their pocketbooks. There was the distinct possibility that women patients might prefer female doctors to male doctors. In the late 1800s, women were extremely modest about their bodies and often found it difficult to be physically examined by a male. Some wondered if a male could truly understand female health problems. Other women, aware of the double standards of the time (respectable women had to have high moral standards, but respectable men did not), felt uneasy about putting themselves and their children into a man's care.

Male doctors knew that a pregnant patient might prefer a woman doctor for childbirth. The delivery of a baby was often a doctor's first contact with a family. The grateful mother would seek that doctor for further births and for the treatment of the whole family. If women doctors were able to make those first important contacts through childbirth, male doctors would lose clients to female doctors. For male doctors, therefore, it made good business sense to discourage women from becoming physicians.

The financial fears were not, of course, openly expressed. Instead, doctors such as F.W. Campbell sneered that women "may be useful in some departments in medicine; but in difficult work, in surgery for instance, they would not have the nerve. And can you think of a patient in a critical case, waiting for half an hour while the medical lady fixes her bonnet or adjusts her bustle?" Underneath the sneers, however, lay unspoken financial fears.

MEDICAL SCHOOL AND EUROPE

When Maude's difficult position became known, there was a public outcry of sympathy for her. Influential people threatened to cut their charitable donations as a result of this shabby treatment, and Maude's ticket of admission suddenly appeared in the mail.

Maude's four years at Bishop's were lonely ones as she was usually the only woman in the class. Although she did not experience the harassment Dr. Augusta Stowe-Gullen had suffered as the first woman to take a medical degree in Canada, she was treated differently because of her sex. She enjoyed the work, however, and was a brilliant student, winning the Senior Anatomy Prize as well the Chancellor's Prize for the best examination results in the final year.

After Maude graduated in 1894, she and her sister, Alice, spent the next three years in Europe. Maude studied medicine at universities in Switzerland and Austria. At that time it was every medical student's dream to study in Vienna, Austria, and it was there that Maude received excellent training in internal medicine and pathology (the study of disease), which she would later put to good use. Maude then interned at a women's hospital in Glasgow, Scotland, and worked in an asylum in Birmingham, England. Tragedy struck, however, before Maude returned to Canada.

ALICE

Alice had travelled to Europe with Maude to study music. While there she was diagnosed as having a manic-depressive disorder. People who have manic depression suffer from extreme moods, which swing from deep depression to wild joy. While in the depression stage, they may feel helpless and worthless, and consider suicide. In the "manic" stage, they may believe they have special connections with famous people or God, or even that they are able to step off high buildings or leave fast-moving vehicles without harm.

Maude spent a great deal of money searching for a cure for Alice, but without success. For the rest of her life Alice remained a chronic invalid who required constant care. As their grandmother had died in 1890, it was up to Maude alone to provide the emotional and financial support her sister would need for forty more years. Maude made sure Alice was cared for in St. Andrews East and then began to make a living.

BACK IN MONTREAL

Maude set up a medical practice for women and children in Montreal in 1897, but she was a scholar at heart and longed to be a part of the academic world. She loved McGill and wanted to be a member of its medical teaching staff.

Dr. Charles Martin, who had been Maude's supervisor at the Montreal General Hospital and was aware of her specialized European training, asked her to study the unusual sounds known as heart murmurs. The research paper she wrote for him was so outstanding that Dr. Martin read it at the Medico-Chirurgical Society. Maude could not present the paper herself, for women were not allowed to become members. After it was presented, however, a motion was quickly passed admitting women to the society and accepting Maude as a new member.

Dr. Martin recommended Maude's work to Dr. John Adami who was the Professor of Pathology at McGill. Dr. Adami set her to work on a piece of medical research that took two years to complete. Her research was so thorough that her paper was presented at the Pathological Society of London in 1900. She was the first woman to have a research paper presented at that society.

Maude continued her medical practice while she worked on the research projects.

CURATOR

Maude's research work was so outstanding that even McGill realized there was something to be gained by using the talents of this exceptional woman. In 1898 she was appointed assistant curator of the McGill Medical Museum, and in 1899 she was promoted to curator.

The museum's specimens should have been an important source of information for medical students in the days before there were colour photographs, videotapes and other modern teaching aids. Disease was not yet studied by means of animal experimentation in laboratories. The medical profession relied upon the study and classification of changes to human tissue and organs caused by disease to provide answers to medical problems. Examples of diseased human organs and body parts, removed after death and preserved in special fluid, should have been vital to medical study and research.

When Maude took over the McGill Medical Museum, however, it was in terrible condition. There were thousands of specimens, some dating back to 1823, but they had not been catalogued or arranged in any sort of systematic way. They were scattered around on shelves and under benches and were useless as teaching aids.

Still carrying on her medical practice, Maude attacked the enormous assignment of organizing the material with her usual thorough and painstaking approach. As there was no established classification method for the specimens, she visited the museums at large American teaching centres. After learning what she could from them, she designed a system for classifying the medical museum specimens and produced a huge catalogue of the McGill collection.

CURATOR AND EDUCATOR

As Maude worked she found many unique and interesting specimens. Her study of the heart specimens in the McGill holdings helped her to become a world authority on congenital (present at birth) heart problems.

Maude was also warm-hearted and unselfish, as medical students soon discovered. Many dropped by the museum to learn from her and to study the fascinating specimens. As a result of Maude's hard work, the medical museum could now take a role in medical education. So many groups of students came to learn from Maude's informal talks and demonstrations that in 1904 McGill asked her to become a demonstrator. Her pathology classes, which used the medical museum's specimens as teaching aids, became an important and compulsory part of a medical student's education.

CURATOR AND AUTHOR

Dr. William Osler was a brilliant physician and medical historian. Maude had met Dr. Osler, who was a fellow Canadian, while he was at work in the United States. He was impressed with young Dr. Abbott and in 1905 asked her to write an article on congenital heart problems to include in his upcoming book entitled System of Medicine. It was an extraordinary honour and Maude did her usual outstanding job. She wrote a thorough, scholarly article that used the findings of over four hundred cases.

The famous Dr. Osler was pleased with Maude's work and wrote to her, "It is by far and away the very best thing ever written on the subject in English—possibly in any language ... For years it will be the standard work on the subject."

From the start, Maude had received little recognition from McGill, in spite of her hard work. Inclusion in Dr. Osler's book now established her as a world authority, but back in Montreal, McGill still refused to formally recognize her achievements. Instead, she was treated as an oddity and as an outsider.

CURATOR AND FOUNDER

In 1907, a fire in the McGill Medical building destroyed many of the medical specimens. Undaunted, Maude began a search for replacement specimens from other medical museums. She had already decided that an association of medical museum curators would be helpful, and in spite of her extraordinary workload, she organized and set up the International Association of Medical Museums. For more than thirty years she was the secretary of the association and the editor of its *Journal of Technical Methods* and its *Bulletin*.

The association, now known as the International Academy of Pathology, has played an important role in the sharing and reporting of medical information. Its letterhead reads "Founded by Maude Abbott in 1906."

HONORARY M.D.

Maude's international reputation grew to the point that McGill could no longer ignore the brilliant scholar in their midst, even if she was female. After all, the achievements of the world-famous Dr. Maude Abbott were enhancing the university's prestige.

In 1910, McGill took the unusual step of awarding Maude an honorary medical degree. While still refusing to admit women into its medical school, McGill now gave her the degree it had refused to let her earn as a student. It was the same medical degree she had been forced to go to Bishop's College to receive.

McGill also appointed her to its medical staff as Lecturer in Pathology. A male physician with such a brilliant reputation would have been given an assistant professorship or even a full professorship. The position of lecturer, however, was at least a step up from museum curator, which was viewed by McGill as a mere sideline position. Along with all her other work, Maude stayed on as curator until 1932.

HARD AT WORK

Maude continued along with her heavy workload and busy schedule. Her fame continued to spread, and young heart specialists came great distances to study with her. She became the editor of the *Canadian Medical Journal* during World War I and was a member of its editorial board until her death.

Maude rejoiced when McGill, the oldest medical school in Canada, finally allowed a few women to study medicine in 1917. Her own sterling reputation probably had some influence on the university's decision. When the five women graduated in 1922, the top McGill medical student was a woman. Maude, who was always interested in medical education for women, helped to found the Federation of Medical Women and also developed and gave a course on the history of medicine at the McGill School of Graduate Nurses.

During World War I, the University of Texas offered Maude an acting professorship. The catch was that she would have to give up the position when the men returned at the end of the war. Maude refused the offer but she spent two years at the Women's Medical College of Pennsylvania. She went there in 1923 as a full professor and as Chairman of Pathology. She had initially refused the invitation, but when the college offered to double her salary, Maude could not resist. Although her workload was usually staggering, much of it paid her nothing. As well, the cost of medical care for Alice often caused her serious financial problems.

In 1925, McGill grudgingly offered Maude the position of assistant professor. The position was not in a regular department but on the sidelines in Medical Research in the McGill University Clinic. There could be no hope of real promotion in this specially created area. Maude may have brilliantly established her place in the world of men, but McGill was not going to be gracious. Her advancement within the university ranks was painfully slow. Over the years she wrote many times requesting promotion, salary increases or additional assistance. Occasionally there were small improvements, but never the promotions that an equally accomplished man would have received.

Nonetheless, Maude returned to the assistant professorship at McGill. She loved McGill, in spite of its shabby treatment of her, and she wanted to be near her invalid sister.

In 1936, Maude's huge book *Atlas of Congenital Heart Disease* was published. It described one thousand cases and formed a solid base of information for modern heart surgery. If there was ever any doubt, this remarkable book confirmed her international reputation as a leading expert in congenital heart problems.

McGILL SAYS NO AGAIN

Maude's enthusiasm, her interest in others, her sense of humour, as well as her brilliance, won her both affection and admiration. At medical meetings, friends and former students crowded around her. Wherever she travelled in North America or Europe, there were friends and admirers eager for a visit from the famous Dr. Abbott.

When she retired in 1936, Dr. Maude Abbott, the acclaimed physician who had made extraordinary contributions to medical science, asked McGill for a favour. She asked that she be retired with the rank of Professor of Medical Research. McGill, which had basked in the international prestige of Maude's brilliant mind and reputation for thirty-seven years, said no.

SIGNIFICANT CONTRIBUTIONS

Upon her retirement, McGill did, however, grant Maude an honorary doctorate (LL.D.). She was also elected an honorary member of the New York Academy of Medicine. Maude continued to work with boundless energy, writing and taking part in lecture tours that included social gatherings in her honour. Altogether, she produced over 140 papers and books. Late in life Maude received a grant from the American Carnegie Foundation to write a textbook on heart disease. She had begun work on the huge project when she suffered a stroke and died at the age of seventy-one.

Two scholarships and a lectureship were established in Maude's memory. A lasting tribute to her was also made by the famous muralist, Diego Rivera. The great Mexican artist included a portrait of Maude in the mural of the fifty most important heart specialists in world history that he created for Cardiological Institute of Mexico in Mexico City. She was the only Canadian *and* the only woman included in Rivera's mural.

In spite of many obstacles, Dr. Maude Abbott made significant contributions to medical science and earned the admiration and respect of scholars and physicians around the world.

Further suggested reading:

Gillett, Margaret. "The Heart of the Matter: Maude E. Abbott, 1869-1940." In Ainley,Marianne Gosztonyi,ed. *Despite the Odds*: *Essays on Canadian Women and Science*. Montreal: Véhicule Press, 1990.

Hacker, Carlotta, *The Indomitable Lady Doctors*. Toronto: Clarke, Irwin, 1974.

Scriver, Jessie Boyd. "Maude E. Abbott." In Mary Quayle Innis, ed. *The Clear Spirit*. Toronto: University of Toronto Press, 1966.

10.1 Award-winning artist, Mary Riter Hamilton.
Mary painted mostly in oils, but she also used
charcoal, pencil and pastel in her battlefield records.

CHAPTER 10

ARTIST

MARY RITER HAMILTON

—— (1873 - 1954) ——

Artists, like other people, must live and yet it is almost impossible to live in Canada by art alone. Not only is it a matter of money, but of appreciation.
— Mary Riter Hamilton

Mary considered the request. She loved France and longed to return to her old haunts. But war had changed Europe. By all accounts, France and Belgium, though now at peace, were bloodied, battered and full of desolation. Would she be overwhelmed by the horror of recent death and destruction?

Yet it was important, Mary thought, to make a record of the places where so many Canadians had died. Through her art, other Canadians, unable to see the sites in person, could share her sense of devastation.

She would return to France, Mary decided. She would accept the task of painting the battlefields of Europe.

EARLY LIFE

Mary Riter was born to Charity Zimmerman Riter and John Riter in 1873. She was born in Teeswater, Ontario, where her father was a saw-mill operator and farmer, but her family soon moved to Clearwater, Manitoba. As a child, Mary loved to paint and draw, but her family lived a pioneer type of life and she was not able to take professional art lessons.

When Mary was sixteen, she married Charles W. Hamilton, and the couple moved to Port Arthur, Ontario (now part of Thunder Bay). Charles ran a successful general store in town, but died in 1893 after only four years of marriage.

Mary, who was financially well-off at that point in her life, returned to Manitoba and began a career in art.

STARTING A NEW CAREER

In 1894, Mary put her skills to practical use and opened a china-painting studio in Winnipeg. Decorated, imported china was expensive and china

101

painting became a popular decorative art in the late 1800s. People discovered that hand painting "blanks" of porcelain cups and plates was a pleasant, artistic occupation.

Mary's studio was a success. She and her students won prizes at exhibitions and found eager buyers for their skilled work. Mary branched into watercolours and by 1898 was teaching that as well as china painting.

Mary herself took art lessons in Toronto, Ontario, from respected artists Mary Hester Reid and George Reid. They had studied in Europe and they encouraged Mary to continue her studies there as well.

FRENCH ACADEMIC STUDY

Paris, France, was the art capital of the world in the late 1800s. Art students from England, the United States, Canada and many European countries flocked there to study. It was the goal of every serious Canadian artist to study at the academies and art schools of Paris. Artists who returned to Canada after French academic training were respected and admired for their knowledge and experience.

Mary decided to join the throngs of other aspiring young artists studying in Europe. She closed her Winnipeg studio in 1901 and started her European art studies with an Italian landscape artist in Berlin, Germany. Her professor told her she had "the gift" and encouraged her to continue her work.

In 1902, Mary rented a small studio in Paris and studied with well-known instructors of the prestigious Vitti Academy. She studied in Paris for almost nine years.

In the 1800s many art classes were closed to women. By the time Mary arrived in Paris, however, women were allowed into the traditional representational art classes. She studied landscape and still-life painting, portraiture and painting from live models. She also took sketching holidays in Spain, Italy and Holland. Mary was a dedicated student who laboured for eight hours each day at her art. She worked in the evenings as well, unless prevented by her friends.

The academies of France often controlled an artist's future. A person whose paintings were exhibited in the yearly Salon of the Academy was acknowledged as a legitimate, professional artist. In 1905, three of Mary's paintings were accepted by the Salon and prominently displayed at the exhibition. After that, her work appeared on a regular basis at the Salon of the Academy. As well, her painting *Les Sacrifices* appeared on the front cover of the popular *Lectures pour tous*, a French art magazine. Mary Riter Hamilton was now part of the European art world.

HOME

Mary was a European success when she returned to Winnipeg to visit her mother in 1906. She showed over seventy of her European oil paintings, sketches and watercolours at exhibitions in Winnipeg and Toronto. The works in this collection, which included landscapes, waterscapes, portraits and still-life studies, were enthusiastically received and a sizable number of them sold. Mary also opened a studio in Winnipeg and taught a large class of art students.

BACK TO PARIS

Mary returned to Paris in the spring of 1907 to continue her studies and European travels. Her painting *Les Pauvres* was accepted for exhibition in the 1909 New Salon in Paris and was also exhibited in the 1915 Panama-Pacific Exhibition in San Francisco.

In 1911, Mary exhibited with the Société Nationale des Beaux-Arts and at the Salon des Indépendants. She was also given special mention in *The Studio*, an international art journal. Critics praised the "personality and distinction" of her work.

Mary often used the people and events of everyday life as subjects for her art. She was influenced by the revolutionary art movement known as Impressionism, which began as a scientific study of light. The painting was often done outdoors rather than inside an art studio, and the artist's brush strokes appeared to be bold and spontaneous. Photographic accuracy was not a goal. Instead, impressionism produced a colourful, vivid and exciting impression that played on the viewer's emotions.

HOME AGAIN

Mary returned to Winnipeg in 1911 because her mother was ill. After her mother's death, nearly 150 of Mary's watercolour and oil paintings were exhibited in Toronto and Ottawa art galleries, at the Art Association of Montreal and in Winnipeg. The exhibitions, held in 1911 and 1912, were a success with the public. One art expert described Mary's work as "masterful in colouring, adroit in draughtsmanship, deft in handling of tones and values, and poetic in treatment of atmosphere and sentiment." Some art critics, however, seemed puzzled. The *Montreal Star* critic said her work was "just a little in advance of the time," but hastened to add that this could be "almost called encouragement." In Winnipeg, Mary's work was criticized for being inconsistent.

In 1912, Mary travelled to Alberta where she painted lakes and mountains. She exhibited this Canadian landscape series in Calgary, then sent them to France where she believed there was an interest in Canadian scenery.

Mary's next stop was the Canadian west coast. To her own surprise, she spent the next five years in Victoria, British Columbia.

NO MAN'S LAND

Germany attacked Belgium in August 1914. Great Britain, an ally of Belgium, responded by declaring war on Germany. As part of the British Empire, Canada found itself at war as well. In the struggle that followed, Germany and Austria fought Russia in Eastern Europe, and Britain, France and Italy in Western Europe. France became the main battlefield for the western Allies, and by January 1915, Canadian troops were there in the front lines.

World War I brought special horrors. Soldiers faced new weapons such as tanks, poison gas, airplanes and flame throwers. On the battlefields, soldiers on both sides often protected themselves by digging deep, muddy trenches and waiting there until instructed to attack. The area that lay between them and the enemy trenches was called "no man's land." When ordered to attack, the soldiers left their trenches and "went over the top" into no man's land. There they tried to dodge the artillery shells and machine gun bullets and swarm into enemy trenches. Many never made it across.

Canadians fought valiantly at battles such as the Somme, Vimy Ridge and Passchendaele, but they paid a high price. By the time the war ended in November 1918, some 60 000 Canadian soldiers had lost their lives, a great many in the muddy tangle of trenches in France and Belgium.

OVERLOOKED

Mary had intended to return to France in 1914, but the outbreak of the war prevented her from doing so. She remained in Victoria, where she opened a studio and gave art lessons. She also painted portraits, and was commissioned to do portraits of British Columbia's lieutenant-governors to hang in Government House. Mary could not sell enough of her work to become financially secure, however. She also missed the supportive atmosphere she had found in France. There was a love of beauty and art among the people there, but in Canada there was little encouragement.

The Canadian War Memorial Fund and the Canadian War Records Office hired official war artists to record Canada's participation in the war. Near the battlefront, the war artists were always male. Back in Canada, however, a few of those who recorded activity on the home front and who produced portraits of military and political figures were female. The artists who were chosen, however, were almost all from Toronto or Montreal. Even when an artist was required to paint the portrait of a war hero in

Vancouver, Mary, an accomplished portrait artist, was overlooked. The commission was given to a male artist based in Eastern Canada.

UNIQUE RECORD

At the end of the war, a magazine called *The Gold Stripe* offered Mary a commission that required her to return to Europe. The magazine, whose proceeds went to the War Amputations Club of British Columbia, hired her to paint the battlefields of Belgium and France. The paintings would appear in *The Gold Stripe*, which published articles and illustrations relating to the war.

In 1919, only six months after the end of the war, Mary returned to Europe. Her special mission was to record the battlefields before all signs of battle were removed. At Vimy, Mary suffered in snow and extreme cold, yet she wrote in one of her letters to *The Gold Stripe* "I want to get the spirit of it ... I feel that it is fortunate that I arrived before it is too late to get a real impression."

It took courage for Mary to live in war-torn Europe. Gangs of criminals roamed the countryside, live ammunition littered the battle zones, and her only neighbours were Chinese labourers hired to clear the

10.2 *Market Among the Ruins of Ypres*, **1920, by Mary Riter Hamilton. In the spring of 1915, Canadian troops at Ypres, Belgium, had been the targets of poison gas. It was a new and dreadful war weapon that caused tremendous suffering.**

10.3 *Sanctuary Wood*, **Flanders, 1920, by Mary Riter Hamilton**

wasted battlefields. She lived alone in a military hut and the food was often inedible. She was "mighty cold and uncomfortable" she wrote in one letter but in another she stated she would not leave until "I finish the work I have come here to do." And so Mary persisted in her task of producing a unique record of Canada's part in The Great War.

THE BATTLEFIELD PAINTINGS

From 1919 to 1922, Mary produced over three hundred battlefield paintings, many completed on site. She had travelled widely in Europe before the war and must have been deeply moved by the wasteland around her. Her grim, impressionistic paintings bear witness to the lasting horrors of war.

Mary focused on battles where Canadian soldiers had fought and died. Her paintings show ruined buildings, scorched woods, overturned tanks and deserted roads scattered through Europe's ravaged countryside.

Yet, as if to emphasize that Canadian soldiers did not die in vain, some of the paintings hint at new life. Some show flowers growing in the trenches beside no man's land, or ordinary people gathering in markets.

The paintings she produced in 1919 were exhibited in Victoria and Vancouver by the War Amputations Club and the Imperial Order of the Daughters of the Empire. As usual, however, her work received more attention in Europe. In 1922, some of Mary's battlefield paintings were

10.4 *Canadian Monument, Passchendaele Ridge*, around 1920, by
Mary Riter Hamilton

exhibited in the Foyer of the Paris Opera as well as at the Société des
Artistes, the Société Nationale des Beaux-Arts, and at the Somme
Memorial Exhibition held in Amiens, France. At the Somme Memorial
Exhibition, Mary was awarded the purple ribbon of Les Palmes
Académiques, the Order of Public Instruction. Her award was as high a
distinction as a woman could receive in France at that time. In 1923, over
a hundred of her battlefield paintings were exhibited in London, England.
While in Europe, Mary received a number of offers to purchase her
collection, but she refused. She had other plans for her battlefield paintings.

BEGINNING OF THE END

After her 1923 exhibition, Mary returned to Paris. There she became ill
and lost the sight in one eye. It is reported that she no longer wished to
paint in her earlier style. The loss of sight in one eye, however, would
have affected her depth perception and hindered her ability to paint
landscapes.

For whatever reason, Mary now began to design, hand paint and
produce "dress accessories." Not only did these prove extremely popular,
but, they earned her a gold medal at the International Decorative Arts
Exhibition. Before the end of the year she had made enough money from
selling her dress accessories to return to Canada with her paintings.

A MEMORIAL TO THE VETERANS

Back in Canada, Mary returned to Winnipeg where she again gave art lessons. She also approached the wife of the local member of Parliament with a plan to donate most of her battlefield paintings to the Canadian government and was put in touch with the Public Archives (now the National Archives) of Canada.

In July 1926 Mary donated 227 of her battlefield works to the Public Archives. She had not created her war paintings to make money, but as a memorial to Canadian soldiers that would remind future generations of the sacrifices they had made. Considering the size of the gift and the recognition Mary had received in Europe, the polite but brief thank-you note from the Public Archives was almost insulting. The award-winning artist was advised that her pictures were being displayed "in a temporary fashion with the posters and war souvenirs."

Mary's work was largely ignored in Canada. There was a growing opposition to war paintings in general by people who believed they glorified war. One newspaper review of a 1927 Winnipeg exhibition of her work rambled on about the location of the exhibit, but did not even mention her battlefield paintings. In 1944, Mary's paintings at the Public Archives were quietly placed in storage.

THE LAST YEARS

Mary stayed in Winnipeg until 1929 when she moved to Vancouver for her health. She opened a teaching studio and in 1933 and 1935 she and her

10.5 *Ravages of War*, around 1920, by **Mary Riter Hamilton**

students exhibited their work. The *Vancouver Province* reviewed the 1935 exhibit and described it as "frankly old fashioned."

Mary gave up teaching after 1939. By 1948, she was having such financial problems that the minister of her church organized a small exhibit of her work in his home. He realized that Mary, who had once been acclaimed and honoured in Europe, would not accept charity. However the cash donations collected as an entrance fee were given to Mary as a gift. The last exhibits of Mary's work during her lifetime were held in the Vancouver Art Gallery in 1949 and 1952.

Mary Riter Hamilton, the award-winning artist who refused to make money from her battlefield paintings, was partially blind, forgotten by the world, and living in poverty when she died in 1954. She was buried in Thunder Bay, Ontario, beside Charles Hamilton, the husband who had died so many years earlier. In her will, she left one of her paintings, *Maternity*, to the city of Thunder Bay. Dated 1906, *Maternity* had been a popular painting, and it was one of Mary's favourites. Childless, she left it to the city where she had lived as a bride, in memory of her husband.

NEW INTEREST

There is now renewed interest in Mary Riter Hamilton and her art. In 1978, the Art Gallery of Greater Victoria held an exhibit of thirty-five of Mary's works, including battlefield paintings, portraits, still lifes and landscapes. In 1989, the War Amputations of Canada, the University of Winnipeg and the National Archives of Canada gave increased recognition to her art when they sponsored the exhibit *No Man's Land: The Battlefield Paintings of Mary Riter Hamilton.*

As one journalist suggested after viewing an exhibit of Mary's work, "Were she a man she would be a world-wide celebrity."

Further suggested reading:

Davis, Angela E. *No Man's Land: The Battlefield Paintings of Mary Riter Hamilton.* Winnipeg: The University of Winnipeg, 1992. [art exhibit catalogue]

11.1 Harriet Brooks, graduation photograph, 1898. Her courses at McGill included English, French, Greek, Latin, Modern History, Mental and Moral Philosophy, Trigonometry and Algebra, Astronomy and Optics, Mechanics and Hydraulics, and Experimental Physics. In four years of study, Harriet stood first in 20 out of the 25 courses.

CHAPTER 11

NUCLEAR PHYSICIST

HARRIET BROOKS PITCHER
—————— (1876 - 1933) ——————

Miss Brooks has a most excellent knowledge of theoretical and experimental Physics and is unusually well qualified to undertake research. Her work on "Radioactivity" has been of great importance in the analysis of radioactive transformations and next to Mme. Curie she is the most prominent woman physicist in the department of radioactivity.

— Lord Ernest Rutherford

Harriet stared out the window as the train rumbled across France. Her stay with friends on the Italian island of Capri had been wonderful, but she missed the challenge of research work.

It would feel good to be back inside a laboratory again, she told herself. And what a laboratory! She smiled with excitement at the thought that she, Harriet Brooks, was on her way to work at the Paris laboratory of Marie Curie, recent winner of the Nobel Prize in physics. Harriet knew it would be a wonderful opportunity.

EARLY LIFE

Harriet Brooks was born in Exeter, Ontario, on 2 July 1876. She was the third child in a family of six girls and three boys. Harriet's father, George Brooks, was a travelling salesman who spent a great deal of time on the road and drinking in saloons. Family members knew that it was Harriet's mother, Elizabeth Warden Brooks, who was the strong parent.

Times were not easy for the Brooks children, for it was hard to feed such a large family on George's small income. Harriet's sister Elizabeth recalled that she never owned a new dress until she became a teacher and could buy one for herself.

The Brooks family also moved frequently until, in 1894, they finally settled in Montreal, Quebec. That same year, Harriet took a daring course of action and entered McGill University.

HARMFUL TO A WOMAN'S HEALTH

Harriet entered McGill only six years after the first woman had graduated from that university. The notion of women receiving higher education was still disputed by many.

In 1873, a former medical professor at Harvard University wrote *Sex in Education*, which solemnly claimed that if the minds of young women were burdened by education, their reproductive systems would be placed under stress. This widely read book, which went through seventeen editions in thirteen years, claimed to document many cases where education seriously damaged the health of young females. Wouldn't higher education, then, also damage the reproductive systems of young males? No one, apparently, asked that question.

As foolish as such claims appear today, they were an effective "for their own good" type of argument that was used to exclude women from universities for years. Many people clung to the traditional view that a young lady should remain demurely at home with her parents until wooed and married by a suitable man.

Those in favour of women attending university argued that it was only fair that women should have equal opportunity. There were also those who believed that women would excel as scientists. They argued that women were naturally suited for scientific research because of their tendency to notice details, their ability to do delicate work with their hands, and their patience. Women university students were still a novelty, then, when Harriet attended and later taught at McGill. In 1900, only 11 percent of Canadian university students were female.

WOMEN AT McGILL

Although women and men at McGill wrote the same examinations and were eligible for the same prizes and medals when Harriet attended university, the women were taught separately. Women students were taught in separate classrooms that had separate waiting rooms, entrances and hallways. Lecturers had to repeat their lectures for the women's class, and some did not wish to do so. As a result, there were fewer courses offered to women. The third- and fourth-year courses, however, were usually co-educational because it was too costly to provide separate lectures for the few women students at that level.

At that time most women university students came from the professional and business families of the middle class. Poorer families could not afford to send their daughters to university, and the wealthiest families often prepared their daughters, not for an intellectual life, but for a life of leisure.

OUTSTANDING

Although her family was poor, Harriet was such an outstanding student that she won scholarships and awards that helped to pay for her education. In her first year at McGill, Harriet won the prize in mathematics and a scholarship that paid her second year's tuition plus $100. In second year, she won the prize in German and a two-year mathematical scholarship worth $125 per year. She focused on physics for the last two years of her degree.

In 1898, Harriet graduated with an honours degree in mathematics and natural philosophy. She also won the Anne Molson medal for outstanding performance in mathematics. After graduation, she was invited to do graduate work in physics at McGill and to join the research group of the outstanding physicist Ernest Rutherford. Rutherford, who later won the Nobel Prize in chemistry, would have an important influence on Harriet's research in nuclear science.

ERNEST RUTHERFORD

The Macdonald Physics Building at McGill was considered to be the best physical laboratory in North America and one of the best-equipped in the world.

Ernest Rutherford, who had been born and raised in New Zealand, began his research on radioactivity in England. Like the scientists Pierre and Marie Curie, Rutherford wanted to discover why materials such as uranium and radium gave out the invisible rays called radiation. In 1898, McGill's international reputation caused him to leave England's Cambridge University and accept a professorship in Canada to continue his research.

Unlike many of the scientists of the time, Rutherford, who would one day be known as the "father of nuclear science," encouraged women scientists and treated them as equals. He believed that "all the young intelligence available" should be trained and used, regardless of gender. However, he would accept only scientists with first-rate research skills into his group. He was also careful, in his lectures and in his written work, to give credit to the work of his students, male or female.

Throughout her career, Harriet turned to Rutherford as someone who would give her professional assistance and advice.

RADIATION STUDIES

Harriet was Rutherford's first graduate student at McGill, and she began by conducting research for him in the field of electricity and magnetism. In 1899, she became staff tutor in mathematics at Royal Victoria College (the women's college at McGill), and she also began research in the puzzling field of radioactivity.

The release of rays from uranium and radium (the element discovered by Marie Curie) was a puzzling phenomenon that could not be explained by the classical physics of the time. If a substance is made up of only one kind of atom that substance is called an element. Elements such as gold, silver and copper can be found in nature in their pure state. Most things in the universe, however, are created from a combination of different elements called a compound. Classical physics held that elements were stable and could not change into other elements. What was happening, then, to the elements uranium and radium when these invisible rays were given off?

In 1900, Rutherford discovered that the element radium gave off radioactive rays as well as a strange radioactive substance that could be moved by air currents. Rutherford called the strange substance "emanation," and Harriet was given the task of discovering what emanation was.

At that time, scientists believed that radioactive elements maintained their identity while the radiation was released. Harriet's research demonstrated that the emanation from radium was a radioactive gas. But the gas (now known as the element radon) did not have the same properties as radium and so was not simply a gaseous form of that element.

Classical physics had long rejected alchemy (chemistry with the goal of changing an element such as lead into gold), but Harriet's research was the first scientific evidence that one element could change—had changed—into another element. This evidence proved to be an important piece in the jigsaw puzzle of modern nuclear science.

Harriet and Rutherford also conducted research work comparing the radiations from the elements thorium, uranium, radium and polonium. As well, they studied the degree to which other substances absorbed radiation. In 1901, Harriet received her master's degree in physics from McGill. The same year, with glowing recommendations from Rutherford, she accepted a position at Bryn Mawr College as fellow in physics.

BRYN MAWR

Bryn Mawr, in the American state of Pennsylvania, was a women's college noted for its high standards and scholarship. Its goal was to educate women to be competitive, independent and never passive. Students were expected to excel and grades from the frequent examinations were publicly posted.

Bryn Mawr also established a graduate school to encourage brilliant students to reach their full potential. As fellow in physics, Harriet joined some sixty to seventy other students in Bryn Mawr's graduate school, where she took courses toward a doctorate degree. While there, she won the President's European Fellowship, which allowed her to spend a year at a leading European university. Although Harriet was worried about her finances, she went to England and spent 1902-03 working with the famous physicist J. J. Thomson at Cambridge University.

TEA TIME AT CAMBRIDGE

Harriet took courses from Thomson and also spent at least twenty-five hours a week on research in the Cavendish Laboratory. Although Thomson's research group was on the leading edge of the study of radioactivity, there were problems. Thomson made only brief appearances in the laboratory, was difficult to communicate with, and appeared to look down on female physics students. A number of times Harriet was forced to write to Rutherford for advice on her experiments when Thomson was no help.

As well, it was a tradition that every two weeks there would be a meeting where one of the research students presented his or her research results. After the presentation there was a formal tea organized by Mrs. Thomson and "one or two ladies connected with the laboratory." No doubt Harriet was expected to help prepare and serve the tea. The assumption that the female members of a professional group would naturally serve refreshments to the male members would have confused Harriet's role within the research group. Was she a gracious servant/helper (serving tea to others) or was she a nuclear physicist (a valued contributor to the real work of the research group)? Even today it is difficult to play both roles successfully in a work situation. This blurring of roles no doubt made female scientists like Harriet feel like outsiders rather than team members.

Although Thomson indicated that Harriet was gifted and skilled in her field, it was probably at Cambridge that Harriet decided not to pursue a doctorate.

MORE DISCOVERIES

Harriet returned to McGill's Royal Victoria College in 1903 as a tutor in mathematics and physics. She also rejoined Rutherford's research group and continued her studies in radioactivity. During her experiments she discovered a phenomenon that was later identified as the recoil of the radioactive atom (a radioactive atom springs back like a fired gun when a particle is ejected). Harriet also discovered that not only was an element transformed during radioactive change, but the product of the change was also radioactive and, in turn, became transformed. The discovery that there was more than one change during this process, known as radioactive

11.2 Early Canadian women in science: Carrie Derrick. In 1921, McGill appointed Carrie Derrick Professor of Morphological Botany. Although it was the first time a professorship had ever been conferred upon a woman in Canada, it was an empty title; the appointment did not carry with it a seat on faculty and it did not give Carrie Derrick an increase in salary. It was, she was told, a "courtesy title".

decay, was Harriet's greatest contribution to physics. She had added yet one more piece to the radioactivity jigsaw puzzle, but it was Rutherford, although he freely gave credit to Harriet's work, who received great acclaim for the discovery.

In 1904, Harriet left McGill and Canada to become tutor in physics at Barnard College.

"YOUR MARRIAGE SHALL BE A RESIGNATION"

Barnard was the women's college of Columbia University in New York City. Harriet taught advanced physics at Barnard until the summer of 1906. She had planned to teach there for the following year as well, but all this changed when she advised Laura Gill, the Dean of the college, of her upcoming marriage to a physics professor at Columbia.

At that time, it was accepted that a woman had to choose between a career and marriage, although Harriet hoped to have both. Male scientists, after all, did not have to choose between the two. The Dean, however, advised her that marriage would end her career at Barnard. Harriet replied in a letter, "I think also it is a duty I owe to my profession and to my sex to show that a woman has a right to the practice of her profession and cannot be condemned to abandon it merely because she marries. I cannot conceive how women's colleges, inviting and encouraging women to enter professions can be justly founded or maintained denying such a principle."

Margaret Malby, who was Barnard's head of physics and an outstanding scientist, wrote to the Dean on Harriet's behalf, praising her personality and abilities, and stating, "She wishes a means of expression, like a man, and the work is near to her heart. Neither you nor I would like to give up our active professional lives ..." The Dean remained firm, however, and responded that "the college is not willing to stamp with approval a woman to whom self-elected home duties are secondary."

Harriet's fiancé had a reputation for being overbearing and somewhat eccentric. In the end, Harriet must have had second thoughts about their future together, and about the atmosphere at the college. Later that summer, she called off her engagement and resigned from Barnard.

MARIE CURIE

That same summer Harriet met Maxim Gorky and his beautiful travelling companion, Maria Andreyeva, while staying at a summer home in the Adirondacks (a mountain resort area in New York State). Gorky was a famous Russian playwright and novelist whose works severely criticized the corruption and decay in Russia before the Russian revolution of 1917. Harriet and Maria Andreyeva became close friends, and in the fall of 1906, Harriet went to Italy as part of Gorky's group and spent time on the Isle of Capri.

She then travelled to Paris and spent part of 1906 and 1907 conducting research for Marie Curie, the scientist who had won the Nobel Prize for physics in 1903. The influential Gorky was fascinated by radioactivity, and he may have arranged the research position for Harriet with Marie Curie. Three articles from the Institute mention Harriet's contributions to radioactivity research while she was there. Marie Curie invited Harriet to stay for another year, but by this time Rutherford had moved from McGill to Manchester University in England. Rutherford prompted Harriet to apply for the important John Harling Fellowship in Physics at Manchester and gave her a glowing recommendation. At the invitation of Rutherford and his wife, Mary, Harriet went to England in 1907. There she found Frank Pitcher waiting.

11.3 Early Canadian women in science: Dr. Maude Abbott. Dr. Abbott (standing in centre) is shown with her friends Dr. Pace and Dr. McLean in Scotland.

MARRIAGE AND THE END OF RESEARCH

Harriet had met Frank Pitcher when she was a student at McGill and he was a laboratory demonstrator working on his Master of Science degree. He became an engineer with the Montreal Water and Power Company and worked his way up to general manager in 1903.

Frank was a persistent admirer of Harriet's, sending her many letters and postcards in 1906 and 1907. In 1907 he travelled to England with the purpose of persuading Harriet to return with him to Montreal. Eventually, he was successful. Harriet married Frank Pitcher in London in July 1907 at the age of thirty-one. She withdrew her application for the John Harling Fellowship and ended her career in science.

Given the expectations and atmosphere of the time, it is not surprising that Harriet finally chose marriage over science. No matter how hard she worked, there would be no upward movement in her career. A doctorate (Ph.D.) was not yet required by universities for male physicists. A woman physicist without her Ph.D., however, would not be offered a senior position at any university. Even a Ph.D. was no guarantee of equality for a woman in science. The best Harriet could hope for was another position of research assistant with someone like Rutherford in England, or another teaching position at one of the women's colleges where there would be limited research and low pay. Perhaps she was tired of the constant struggle for acceptance and recognition in a field where women were seldom welcomed. There would also have been great pressure on Harriet from friends, relatives and society as a whole, to marry and produce children.

Harriet and Frank returned to live in Montreal, but she always remained friends with the Rutherfords. She must therefore have rejoiced when Rutherford and scientist Frederick Soddy put the jigsaw puzzle pieces together in 1908 and discovered the secret of radioactivity.

RADIOACTIVITY AND NUCLEAR SCIENCE

Rutherford and Soddy, using the discoveries of scientists such as Harriet Brooks, realized that as they learned more about the strange phenomenon of radioactivity, they were also learning more about the structure of the atom itself. They discovered that radioactivity is something that was coming from inside the atom. When an element is giving out radioactivity, part of the element is shooting out, and the radioactive part is itself changing into a different element. As a result of this discovery, Rutherford and Soddy won the Nobel Prize for chemistry in 1908.

Scientists had thought that the atom could not be divided any further. However, in 1911 Rutherford discovered that the atom itself consists of even smaller particles and that it is made up of tiny electrons surrounding a larger core called a nucleus. Later the nucleus was discovered to consist of protons and neutrons held together by an extremely powerful force. Rutherford rejected the idea that the energy stored inside the atom's nucleus could be released and put to use. At that time, nuclear physics remained a fascinating theoretical science rather than one that could serve a practical purpose.

Not until 1938 did other scientists discover that the tremendous energy stored inside the atom, known as nuclear energy or atomic energy, could be released by a process known as nuclear fission. Most of the energy released by nuclear fission takes the form of heat, while the rest takes the form of radiation. Nuclear fission was used in atomic bombs at the end of World War II. A nuclear power plant also uses the huge amount of heat energy produced by nuclear fission to change water into steam. The steam is then used to produce electricity.

Early scientists such as Harriet Brooks and Ernest Rutherford, who had set out to study the puzzling phenomenon of radioactivity, were the pioneers of modern nuclear science. Piece by piece, their discoveries provided the groundwork for later scientific breakthroughs.

JOY AND SORROW

Harriet and Frank Pitcher lived in a wealthy area of Montreal and vacationed in the Laurentian Mountains, ninety-five kilometres north of the city. There they owned over four hundred hectares of land that

included three small lakes, a summer home and a farm. With three children, many interesting house guests, and volunteer work in various women's organizations, Harriet at first had a contented, busy life. Nieces who frequently visited the Pitchers fondly recalled the happy times there and Harriet's warm and understanding personality.

Beginning in the 1920s, however, a series of tragedies struck the family. Harriet's eldest son died of spinal meningitis three days after his fourteenth birthday. In 1929, Barbara, Harriet's only daughter and an eighteen-year-old student at McGill, mysteriously disappeared on campus. Seventeen days later her body was found in a river. The coroner did not suspect foul play and rendered a verdict of "found drowned." Less than two years later, Harriet's last child became ill with tuberculosis. Fortunately, he recovered after spending a year at a sanatorium.

11.4 Early Canadian Women in science: Maud L. Menten, PhD in biochemistry. Maud gained international recognition when she and another scientist developed a revolutionary biochemical concept known as the *Michaelis-Menten Equation*.

Harriet herself died on 17 April 1933, at the age of fifty-six. At the time of her death, her lengthy illness was described as a "blood disorder." Like Marie Curie, however, Harriet probably died of leukemia brought on by her unprotected exposure to radiation when she was a young nuclear physicist.

INVISIBLE KILLER

In the pioneer days of nuclear science, scientists were not aware that radioactive material was dangerous. Today, people who work with such material protect themselves from the invisible rays and the dust those rays cling to with special clothing and equipment; they *never* touch radioactive material with their bare hands. Marie Curie, Ernest Rutherford and Harriet Brooks, however, took no precautions whatsoever. Marie Curie and her husband, Pierre, had observed that handling radium caused terrible skin damage, but at the time no one realized there were more deadly dangers.

Early scientists knew that laboratories and people became radioactive, but only complained because the radioactivity distorted the electroscope readings for their own experiments. Even today, Marie Curie's notebooks are still too radioactive to be touched without protective clothing.

One of Harriet's earliest research projects for Rutherford involved studying and working with the radioactive element radon, which we now know is extremely dangerous. During the radioactive decay process of radon, some of the radioactive atoms would have passed into Harriet's bloodstream and she would have also inhaled radioactive dust particles. It was later that scientists discovered that radiation destroyed human bones and blood by slowing down or killing living cells. Radiation sickness, as it became known, affected thousands of laboratory workers in Europe and North America in the 1920s. In Harriet's case, it probably caused her death.

OVERLOOKED

Although Harriet was one of Canada's first researchers in the study of radioactivity, her contributions to science have been largely overlooked. Her discoveries are often credited to other scientists, and her name rarely appears in Canadian science books.

Perhaps one day Harriet Brooks Pitcher will be recognized for her significant discoveries in the field of nuclear science.

Further suggested reading:

Rayner-Canham, Marelene F. and Geoffrey W. Rayner-Canham. *Harriet Brooks: Pioneer Nuclear Scientist.* Montreal & Kingston: McGill-Queens University Press, 1992.

Rayner-Canham M.F., and G.W. Rayner-Canham. "Harriet Brooks, 1876-1933: Canada's First Woman Nuclear Scientist". In Marianne Gosztonyi Ainley, ed. *Despite the Odds:Essays on Canadian Women and Science*. Montreal: Véhicule Press, 1990.

12.1 Millie and friends in front of J.F. Lord's store, photograph by Mille Gamble. Mille is second from the left.

12.2 Women and girls of the Tryon Baptist Church Mission Band at work, photograph by Millie Gamble.

CHAPTER 12

PHOTOGRAPHER

MILLIE GAMBLE

—— (1887 - 1986) ——

"She made a history of us as kids. If anything was going on, Millie was there."

— **Adelaide Ives Wood**

"All right now, Millie girl, you can look."

Millie opened her eyes and stared with surprise at the box on the kitchen table.

"It's a present for you," her uncle continued. "I know it's not your birthday and all, but, well, I think it's something that you'll like."

Flushing with pleasure at the unexpected present, Millie gave her uncle a quick kiss on the cheek. Then she opened the box and gasped. It was a camera! She didn't know anyone back home who had a camera.

"Oh, it's a wonderful gift!" she exclaimed.

Her uncle chuckled and gave her a little hug. "Should keep you busy for a little while, Millie girl."

EARLY LIFE

Millie Gamble was born in Alberton, Prince Edward Island, on 17 January 1887. She was one of three girls born to Janie Nelder Gamble and Thomas Gamble. Millie attended Prince of Wales College in Charlottetown, Prince Edward Island, where she received her teacher's licence in 1904.

That summer while visiting her relatives in Truro, Nova Scotia, Millie received a Ray No. 1 camera as a gift. She immediately began taking photographs and became part of an amateur photography craze that was sweeping North America.

CAMERA OBSCURA

Since early times, people had attempted to make images of themselves and the world around them. Only the wealthy, however, could afford to hire portrait painters.

In the 1700s the growing European middle class also wanted an affordable way to preserve likenesses of themselves and their loved ones.

Painted miniature portraits were not as costly as large portraits but they were still expensive.

Inventors began to investigate the possibilities of using light to produce a picture cheaply and without special skills. For centuries, people have known that if there is a small hole in the wall of a darkened room, an image of the outside world will be thrown up on the opposite wall. The image will be smaller, upside down and dim. This phenomenon, known as the camera obscura (Latin for "dark room" or "dark chamber") was put to use by some European artists in the 1700s. These artists used small wooden boxes to produce images that they could trace onto paper. A small movable lens at front of the box focused the image on a mirror inside the box. The mirror then reflected the image, right side up, onto a glass screen on the top of the box and the image was then traced.

A PERMANENT PICTURE

A camera obscura was helpful, but people wanted to turn the image that it produced into a permanent picture. Could the same light that produced the camera obscura image also be used fix the image permanently onto a surface?

People had observed that light changed certain materials. Some faded, but others, such as certain silver compounds, darkened when they were exposed to light. This led to the idea that it might be possible to use such compounds to permanently imprint an image on a surface exposed to light rays. The first practical process was invented by French artist Louis Daguerre. His invention was announced in 1839, and by the early 1840s the pictures called daguerreotypes were being produced in Canada. In 1842, over forty years before Millie's birth, there was a daguerreotypist working in Prince Edward Island. Daguerreotypes created a sensation, but the process was slow, complicated and expensive. As well, it did not produce a negative, so it was impossible to make copies of a daguerreotype.

WRITING WITH LIGHT

Daguerreotypes were replaced with wet-plate photography, invented in 1851, which produced larger pictures as well as negatives. Now using a camera could be more profitable because an endless number of prints (positives) could be produced from the original image (negative). The product of this negative-to-positive process was called a photograph, which means "writing with light" in Greek.

In wet-plate photography, a glass plate was coated with silver salts and a sticky fluid called collodion. When a picture was taken, the glass plate inside the dark camera was exposed to light for a few seconds. The plate

12.3 The Ives family fishing, photograph by Mille Gamble

was then developed with chemicals into a negative by the photographer and treated with a fixing agent. Since the collodion had to remain moist during the exposure and developing stages, it was necessary for the photographer to process the photographs as soon as the pictures were taken, while the glass plates were still wet.

Travelling photographers had to carry a portable dark room, a variety of chemicals, glass plates, dishes and tanks, as well as a heavy camera and a tripod with which to hold it steady while the picture was taken. As a result, many photographers began opening their own photography studios in order to avoid moving the heavy equipment around. Now, at last, many people could afford to buy a likeness of themselves and their loved ones.

Women photographers sometimes set up studios in their own home so that they could keep an eye on their children as they worked at their profession. The few women photographers in daguerreotype or wet-plate photography usually did portrait work. Customers often came to them, however, because they believed a woman photographer would be more sensitive and patient with both adults and children.

During the 1870s the revolutionary dry-plate photography process was introduced. The exciting world of photography soon opened up to thousands of people like Millie Gamble.

A TECHNOLOGICAL BREAKTHROUGH

In 1871, a British physician discovered that gelatin, unlike collodion, did not harm the silver salts when it dried on a glass plate. Using the dry-plate method, photographers no longer had to develop their pictures as soon as they were taken. In fact, photographers could now give the plates to others to develop, and the photo-finishing industry was born.

There were other advantages to the dry-plate method, as well. The exposure time was greatly reduced, so it was no longer necessary to place a camera on a tripod to avoid "camera shake." Cameras could now be hand-held. Moreover, a photographer no longer needed to be an expert chemist; by the 1880s commercially manufactured glass plates came ready to use from the factory. If stored properly, the plates would hold their sensitivity to light for a long period of time. The photographer simply loaded the unexposed plates into the camera in a darkroom. After the pictures were taken, the exposed plates were either sent away to be developed, or else brought back to the darkroom for developing, fixing, washing and drying.

The dry-plate method of photography was also much cheaper, so photography was no longer a pastime for only the rich. It is no wonder then, that with the introduction of the dry-plate method, there was a huge increase in the number of professional and amateur photographers in Europe and North America. By 1891, there were 1277 professional photographers in Canada, 135 of whom were female. However, the number of Canadian amateur photographers, male and female, was far greater. Now, for the first time in history, it was easy for ordinary people to make a visual record of the everyday events of their lives.

WOMEN AND PHOTOGRAPHY

Studio portraits often showed women stiffly posed beside their husbands and children. These photographs "wrote with light," but the "writing" had little to do with reality. The elaborate, sometimes exotic backdrops of ornate furniture and oriental rugs were usually supplied by the studios and told the viewer little about the subjects' homes.

The subjects were usually placed in standard and unimaginative poses. Sometimes women stood to reveal the lines of their best dresses. Sometimes, if it was decided that a woman's feet were too large, she sat with her feet tied back to the chair. Dainty shoes pushed onto pieces of wood, were stuck out from beneath her long skirts to give her feet what was thought to be a more delicate, and therefore more "ladylike" appearance.

Until the 1880s there were few professional women photographers; women were viewed as consumers rather than producers of photography. At precisely this time, however, women were forcing society to change its view of what was right and proper for "the fair sex." They were becoming more visible by leaving their homes to attend university or enter the labour

12.4 Berry-picking, photograph by Millie Gamble. Millie is second from the left.

12.5 Millie's nieces, Adelaide and Hope Ives, playing with their toys, photograph by Millie Gamble.

force. Some were questioning the way society controlled women by telling them what activities were, and were not, feminine.

Women, therefore, responded with enthusiasm to the new technology of photography. When a woman such as Millie Gamble owned a camera, she herself selected the images from her life that would be preserved. They were not, however, images that were widely published.

IMAGES OF WOMEN

From the very beginning of the industry, photographs of women were frequently used in newspapers, books, pornography and advertising. These images of women, however, were almost always produced by and selected by men. Women did not have a way to widely distribute their photographic images of themselves, their work, and their experiences. Ironically, the new technology of photography, which women welcomed as early as the 1880s, was often used in the media to perpetuate the stereotype of women as incompetent. The Eastman Kodak Company, which cleverly created its business empire by claiming to simplify photography, often advertised with photographs of young women using Kodak cameras. The real message of the advertisement was "So simple, even a woman can use it."

Fortunately, Millie Gamble and others like her took photographs of the world around them for their own pleasure and to select the images *they* wished to preserve. All photographs are a short cut to the past, but Millie's photos recorded what the stiff studio portraits and the glib advertisements did not. Millie's camera showed the activities of ordinary women and children, often in everyday surroundings and everyday clothing. Like a well-written diary, Millie's photographs give the viewer a sense of what it was like to be a woman in the early 1900s.

MILLIE'S PHOTOS

In the autumn of 1904, Millie began teaching in the primary room of the Tryon Consolidated School in Prince Edward Island. Although interest in photography had swept through Prince Edward Island, for Tryon the closest professional photographer was located in Charlottetown. Seventeen-year-old Millie, who had started taking photographs for something to do, was also asked by mothers to take pictures of babies and school children.

Around the time that Millie began to record the near and the familiar in Prince Edward Island, the Island's most famous inhabitant, author Lucy Maud Montgomery, was already a part of the amateur photography trend. As early as 1899, Maud Montgomery was taking photographs of the places she loved in and around Cavendish, the model for her fictional Avonlea.

12.6 Millie's nieces, Hope and Adelaide Ives, sitting on sacks in a field, photograph by Millie Gamble

Millie's photos, on the other hand, were most often of people. Her sense of humour and her love of life must have set her subjects at ease, for they have a relaxed and natural appearance that is unusual for the time. Millie recorded the day-to-day activities of her sister Helen Gamble Ives, and her nieces Hope and Adelaide Ives, as well as those of other women in Tryon. Millie took an active part in church, school and community affairs, and her photographs record the details of a woman's life in rural Canada.

MILLIE AND HER RAY NO. 1

Millie's Ray No. 1 camera was a dry-plate camera with glass plates that were 10.16 centimetres by 12.7 centimetres (4" by 5") in size. The Ray No. 1 was a type of portable amateur camera known as a "cycle camera" because it could be attached to a bicycle on outings. The manufacturer, the Ray Camera Company of Rochester, New York, eventually became a part of the Eastman Kodak Company.

Millie set up a darkroom in the kitchen pantry to develop her photographs. It was essential, however, to place the developed prints under running water to rinse off the chemicals, and there was no running water in Millie's house. Millie devised a simple but effective system to wash the prints at the Gamble water pump. She put them in a can with a hole in it and placed another can, also with a hole in it, on top. She then positioned the cans under the water spout and pumped by hand until the chemicals were washed from the prints.

Millie continued to be interested in photography, but when she left Prince Edward Island in 1919 to study nursing at the Winnipeg General Hospital, she left her Ray No. 1 behind.

12.7 Women and children working in a field, photograph by Millie Gamble

LATER YEARS

Millie graduated as a nurse from the Winnipeg General Hospital in 1922. She returned to Tryon, where she did hospital and private nursing until she retired in 1949. After retirement Millie cared for her aging mother and continued to be an active member of the community, and in particular of the Tryon Women's Institute.

Millie's photographs, known as the Gamble Collection, are now at the Public Archives of Prince Edward Island. Millie was living with Adelaide Ives Wood, the niece she had so often photographed, when she made her gift to the provincial government.

Millie Gamble died on 13 February 1986 at the age of ninety-nine. Today, her photographs continue to "write with light" those otherwise unrecorded events of a woman's life in rural Canada.

Further suggested reading on women and photography:

Pedersen, Diana and Martha Phemister. "Women and Photography in Ontario, 1839-1929." In Marianne Gosztonyi Ainley, ed. *Despite the Odds: Essays on Canadian Women and Science.* Montreal: Véhicule Press, 1990.

Evans, Barbara. "'We Just Lived It As It Came Along' Stories from Jessie's Albums." In Catherine A. Cavanaugh and Randi R. Warne, eds. *Standing on New Ground: Women in Alberta.* Edmonton: University of Alberta Press, 1993.

CHAPTER 13

FIRST WOMAN MEMBER OF PARLIAMENT

AGNES MACPHAIL
———— (1890 - 1954) ————

Perhaps if I owed my father the ability to get into Parliament, I owed to my mother the ability to stand it when I got there.

— Agnes Macphail

As Agnes Macphail paused during her speech, a heckler in the front row shouted, "Aw, why don't you get a husband?"

Agnes walked to the edge of the platform and pointed at the man. "Get up!" she ordered. The crowd echoed her command, and the man reluctantly got to his feet. "I suppose you're married," said Agnes; the heckler mumbled that he was.

Agnes looked at the crowd and said, "Now, I'd bet he wasn't like this when his wife married him ten years ago." She looked back at the heckler and added in triumph, "What guarantee have I that anybody I married now wouldn't turn out like you in ten years?"

The crowd howled with laughter, and the humiliated man sank back down in his seat.

It was foolish to heckle Agnes Macphail.

EARLY YEARS

Agnes Campbell Macphail was born 24 March 1890, in a log farmhouse in Grey County, Ontario. Grey County is located south of Lake Huron's Georgian Bay. The eldest of three girls, Agnes felt that her own strong determination and her belief in public service were traits she owed to her Scottish ancestors, the Campbells and the Macphails. Her mother, Henrietta Campbell Macphail, was a strong woman who believed females should face trouble and pain without whining or tears. Her father, Dougal Macphail, was first a farmer and then an auctioneer who was well known for his persuasive powers and his quick wit. Agnes inherited these personality traits, and they would serve her well during her political career. She also loved and idolized Jean Black Campbell, her "brave and bonny" grandmother, who had been a pioneer in Grey County.

The Macphail farm was a favourite meeting place, and Agnes loved to listen to the farmers discuss their crops and their problems and the politics of the day. She grew up believing that farm people were fine, honest, hardworking people, and she never lost that belief.

A TEACHER

Agnes became a teacher and taught in small country schools in Ontario and Alberta. A lively, outgoing young woman, she enjoyed teaching and boarding with farm families, and she enjoyed discussing politics and farm issues. Yet although Agnes was interested in politics, she was not a suffragist and did not take part in the women's suffrage movement.

13.1 Agnes Macphail. Agnes was taught by her grandmother Campbell that it was the duty of the strong to champion and protect the weak.

13.2 An Alberta school in 1908. A a young woman, Agnes taught in small county schools in Ontario and Alberta. Agnes liked the out-going people of Canada's midwest.

The suffrage movement fought long and hard for women's right to vote and stand for political office, and eventually was successful in enabling women to do more than just talk about politics. By late April 1918, women from the western provinces, Ontario and Nova Scotia had won the right to vote in their provincial elections.

In May 1918, the federal government passed a law giving Canadian women the right to vote in federal elections. The following year, the federal government passed a law giving women the right to run for federal office. Immediately, politicians began to seek the support of this large group of new voters. Like the suffragists, the politicians believed that women would vote as a united group for political parties that promised to reform society.

A NEW CAREER

At this time, a number of small political parties in Canada were demanding social reforms such as more funding for education and health care and labour laws to protect workers. As these smaller parties, such as the United Farmers of Ontario, were always trying to expand their membership, they often encouraged women to join. The social issues these parties fought for were issues that many women supported. It was therefore not surprising that Agnes Macphail, who believed in social reform all her life, became a member of the United Farmers of Ontario.

What was surprising to some, however, was that in 1921 the United Farmers of Ontario chose Agnes as their candidate to run in the federal election for the constituency of South-East Grey (later Grey-Bruce). Agnes beat nine men for the position, and after her victory some party members demanded that she withdraw so that a male could become the candidate instead. Although even her family had doubts about her decision to enter politics, Agnes refused to withdraw.

The 1921 federal election was the first chance Canadian women had to run for Parliament. Of the four women candidates who stood for office in that election, only Agnes Macphail won. Her grasp of the issues, her determination, and her appeal to audiences brought her victory and a place in the history books as the first female member of Parliament. Agnes later wrote, "If I had known before I entered public life what it meant for a woman to invade a man's world I wouldn't have been able to face it." As she set off to Ottawa, however, she had no idea of the ordeal that lay ahead in the House of Commons.

THE HOUSE OF HORRORS

Since its beginning, the House of Commons had been a select male club. In 1919, when the laws changed to allow women to run for federal office,

133

many members of Parliament were hostile to the idea of women in the House. Agnes had expected other women to join her there. Instead, she was the only female member for the first fourteen years of her parliamentary career.

Resentful male colleagues let Agnes know that becoming a member of Parliament was, in their opinion, improper behaviour for a female. Some of them rudely left whenever she rose to speak in the House. Some put on an air of exaggerated courtesy to make her feel like an outsider. Others jeered at her and criticized everything she did.

Agnes had hoped to be treated like any other member of Parliament, but this was not to be. As the lone woman, she stood out and received a great deal of attention. It was not, however, the kind of attention that focused on her skills and ability or on the issues she supported. It was the kind that focused on what made her different from the others. Agnes later recalled, "The misery of being under observation and being unduly criticized is what I remember most vividly about those first few months."

In the corridors, in the House of Commons itself and even in the House dining room, Agnes was constantly gawked at. So many people stared at her in the dining room that she lost over five kilograms in the first month and began to eat in downtown Ottawa restaurants instead. Her desk mate for ten years in the House of Commons grew so tired of visitors constantly staring and pointing at their section of the House that he once referred to himself as the "man in a cage."

Agnes recalled, "I couldn't open my mouth to say the simplest thing without it appearing in the papers. I was a curiosity, a freak. And you know how the world treats freaks."

Agnes often found herself forced into a role that had little to do with her as a person. She had not campaigned on women's rights, yet she was always expected to express an opinion on "women's issues" as though she were suddenly the spokesperson for Canadian women everywhere.

LADIES AND GENTLEMEN OF THE PRESS

Agnes was a warm, outgoing thirty-one-year-old woman with a zest for living, yet the press focused on her direct manner of speaking and portrayed her as "a cantankerous old maid." Yet the same critics would never have described a thirty-one-year-old, forthright, unmarried male as "a cantankerous old bachelor." She was particularly disappointed with the female reporters who went out of their way to make her early political life difficult. At that time, female reporters were usually assigned to write for society columns, and their accounts of Agnes's work on the great social issues of the day were careless and vague. They chose, rather, to focus much of their attention on the trivial issue of her clothing. There were no practical guidelines for the first woman member of Parliament on any topic. As far as clothing was concerned, Agnes, surrounded by a sea of business suits in Parliament, often wore a simple, blue wool dress. The dress was ridiculed by female reporters, as was her decision to sit bare-headed in the House. "Our kind of lady would prefer to see you wear a hat," sniffed one.

Male reporters could be equally hostile. One reporter asked her, "Do you think it is possible to go into political life and yet keep radiant and untarnished the inner shrine of a woman's modesty, delicacy and sensitiveness?" Agnes, in her direct way, replied "I surely do. Public life broadens, not blunts a woman's make-up."

In spite of her intense unhappiness during her first session of Parliament, Agnes drew upon the toughness and tenacity she had inherited from her mother. She stuck it out in the "man's world" and learned to love Parliament and enjoy her work as a member.

HARDWORKING REFORMER

During Agnes's first term in office, her party fell apart. After that, she did not run as a candidate for any political party, choosing instead to run as an independent. Several times the Liberals promised her a cabinet position if she would run as their candidate, but she refused. Running in a federal election without the support of a political party was not easy; nonetheless Agnes won four more federal elections as a result of her hard work in Parliament and in the riding she represented.

13.3 Agnes fought hard for Canada's rural population. She said of farm families, "They know just a little bit more about hard work and about saving than any other large group of people ... and I think it is not going too far to say that they are the bedrock of our whole national life."

13.4 Agnes grew up on a farm and knew a farm woman's work was never done.

13.5 Agnes once said in the House of Commons, "It is true that the farmers work hard; it is true that their days are long and their pay is poor. But it is also infinitely true that the farm woman's day is longer and her pay poorer."

Remembering the rural voters who re-elected her time and time again, Agnes championed the rights of farmers everywhere. She was a strong supporter of the rural co-operative movement, whose members banded together to run businesses and share the profits. She also put into action her grandmother Campbell's belief that it is the duty of the strong to help and protect the weak. In 1921, there was no crop failure insurance for farmers, no unemployment insurance, no family allowance, no old age pension, and no medical insurance plans. Throughout her career, Agnes fought for the social reform legislation that we take for granted today such as old age pensions and equal pay for men and women who work at the same jobs. In one of her speeches in the House, Agnes declared that the men who were against equal pay for equal work "are used to women doing a lot of work [in the home] for nothing, so they do not see why in factories and other places of employment they should not do the same."

It was not easy to bring in change. Many members of Parliament were against social reform legislation, and politicians who had expected women to vote as a group for social reform were soon proved wrong. Women did not vote as a group for female candidates or for particular issues any more than men did. Politicians quickly discovered they did not necessarily have to promise and deliver social change in order to win female votes in their ridings.

Agnes was a pacifist and spoke out against war and the way school textbooks glorified wars and battles. She also protested against military cadet training for boys in elementary and high schools. It glorified war, she believed, and made it appear exciting to boys and young men. She was a strong supporter of the League of Nations, (the predecessor of today's UN), and in 1929 she became the first Canadian woman delegate to the League of Nations Conference in Geneva.

Prison reform was, however, Agnes's greatest achievement. She repeatedly drew Parliament's attention to the deplorable conditions in Canada's dirty, rat-infested jails, demanding an end to the flogging of prisoners, the use of untrained and sadistic prison guards and the neglect of insane prisoners who were left howling in their cells.

After years of protest on her part, a royal commission was finally appointed in 1935 to investigate Canada's prison system. The resulting Archambault Report confirmed what Agnes had been saying all along: Canada's prisons were a disgrace. Chief Justice Archambault mailed a copy of his report to her with the words: "To Miss Agnes Macphail, M.P., courageous pioneer and untiring worker on behalf of prison reform in Canada."

TO MARRY OR NOT TO MARRY

Agnes always wanted the freedom to live her life as a distinct individual. The idea of having to fit into the life a husband had chosen for himself did not appeal to her independent spirit. Politics took up all of her time, and it did not seem possible to continue as a member of Parliament, a job she now loved, and find time to spend with a husband and children.

The press often portrayed her in photographs and reports as severe, but her friends knew her as someone who brought a room alive when she entered. In her busy private life she laughed and danced and partied and enjoyed meeting people from all over the world. Men admired her tall, graceful figure, her wavy brown hair, her rich voice, her flashing wit and her outgoing personality.

Agnes was much in demand as a speaker and made many friends as she travelled across Canada and the United States on speaking tours. She had suitors and admirers in both countries, yet she could not bring herself to marry. Agnes, who loved children, contented herself with surprising her nieces with generous gifts. However, when she handed over her papers to the National Archives of Canada, she deliberately included a few love letters. She did not like the press's image of her as a cold and loveless spinster, and she did not want to be remembered that way.

Agnes was impatient with members who wanted to deny women equal rights while gushing that "a woman is the angel of the home." During one debate in the House she responded, "I do not want to be the angel of any home; I want for myself what I want for other women, absolute equality. After that is secured then men and women can take turns at being angels." She added wryly, "I remember that last year an honourable member ... called a woman an angel and in the next breath said that men were superior. They must therefore be gods."

DEFEATS AND VICTORIES

By her fifth term Agnes was an experienced member of Parliament and respected by all parties for her hard work, integrity and debating skill. Even the press was sometimes kind and wrote about "her natural friendliness" and "her interest in human beings." All the same, after nineteen years in office, she was defeated for the first time in the federal election of 1940.

Agnes had worked tirelessly for her riding of Grey-Bruce, but by this time Canada was fighting World War II. Although she supported Canada's war effort, her earlier pacifist comments worked against her at the polls. As well, a huge snow storm in Grey County closed many country roads on election day and kept large numbers of Agnes's rural supporters from reaching the polling stations to vote.

Agnes, now suddenly out of a job, had to find a new source of income. She became a member of the Co-operative Commonwealth Federation (CCF) party and was elected to the Ontario legislature in 1943 for the riding of East York. She was, again, the only female member. Agnes was defeated in 1945 but was re-elected for that riding by a large majority in 1948.

The Ontario legislature with its 90 members seemed small to Agnes after her many years in the 245-member House of Commons. The issues, however, were much the same. In spite of ill health, she continued to champion the underprivileged, arguing for improved public school education, universal hospital insurance, improved reform institutions, equal pay for the equal work of men and women, and an increase to the supplement for old age pensions.

Agnes's political career ended with her defeat in the Ontario election of 1951. She did not have a pension and worried that she would die in poverty; although many believed she would make an excellent senator, she was not appointed. Agnes Macphail suffered a third heart attack and died on 13 February 1954, at the age of 63.

IN MEMORIAM

As the first woman to sit in the House of Commons, Agnes had blazed the trail for other women in federal politics. Immediately after her death, the five women members of Parliament and the four women senators who had followed in her footsteps arranged for a bronze bust to be made of Canada's first woman member of Parliament. This memorial to Agnes Macphail, a woman of integrity who championed Canada's less fortunate, stands in the House of Commons she loved.

Further suggested reading:

Stewart, Margaret, and Doris French. *Ask No Quarter*. Toronto: Longmans, Green and Company, 1959.

French, Doris. "Agnes Macphail." In Innis, Mary Quayle,ed. *The Clear Spirit*. Toronto: University of Toronto Press, 1966.

Norcross, E. Blanche. *Pioneers Every One*. Toronto: Burns & MacEachern Limited, 1979.

14.1 Blue Monday on Keewaydin Island, Ontario. Monday was the traditional wash day because most people changed their clothes once a week on Sunday. Doing the laundry was usually a woman's most hated task because it was hot, heavy, hard work.

CHAPTER 14

POET AND AUTHOR

EDNA JAQUES
—— (1891 - 1978) ——

Although I wouldn't trade places with the queen, I wouldn't go back over the trail I've come for a million dollars in guinea gold.

— Edna Jaques

Edna and Clyde hesitated outside the front door of the Moose Jaw Times. Clyde held three of Edna's poems, carefully rolled up and tied with a blue hair ribbon. He looked down at his sister, whose face was pinched with fear, and patted her shoulder. "Don't be so scared, Edna. I'll take the poems in and you won't have to say a word. Just stand there and nod." Fourteen-year-old Edna forced a smile.

"Here, you hold the poems while I dust off my pants," Clyde added innocently. As Edna's hand closed around the poems, Clyde threw open the door, pushed her inside the newspaper office, then pulled the door shut. Edna frantically yanked the knob without success; Clyde was pulling from the other side.

With no means of escape, Edna slowly turned around to face the imposing-looking man who sat behind a large wooden desk.

"Have you something there for me?" the big man asked.

OFF TO SASKATCHEWAN

Edna Jaques (pronounced "Jakes") was born 17 January 1891, in Collingwood, Ontario. In 1902 her father, who had been the captain of a Great Lakes passenger ship, made a startling announcement. Charles Jaques told his family they were leaving Collingwood to homestead in Saskatchewan. Edna's mother, Nellie O'Donohue Jaques, fainted at the news.

Edna's family sold their house and most of their possessions, including bicycles, doll carriages and their mother's prized piano, before they set off for the midwest. Her mother, who loved Collingwood's tree-lined streets and her comfortable home there, wept as they left for an uncertain future.

BRIERCREST

The Jaques family settled on a homestead that was forty kilometres southeast of Moose Jaw, Saskatchewan. They were the first settlers in the area and Edna's mother called their place Briercrest.

Like many settlers, they built the barn first and lived in it while the little house was being built. When the homestead house was completed, the children slept upstairs in the tiny attic on homemade mattresses stuffed with straw. Edna's older brothers, Bruce and Clyde, slept at one end, and Edna and her younger sisters, Madge and Arlie, slept at the other. On winter mornings the children woke with red noses and hair that was white with frost.

THE MUSTANGS

Settlers on the prairie did not have the backbreaking job of cutting down trees and removing tree stumps before the fields could be planted. Still, the prairie sod was tough. Held together by the millions of entangled sagebrush, grass and brier roots known as "prairie wool," it had to be laboriously turned over and broken up before it could be seeded. Edna's father, however, knew nothing about farming. Charles Jaques's first mistake was to buy wild Montana mustangs to pull the plough. Mustangs were the small, swift horses descended from horses brought to North America by the early Spanish explorers. The four mares Edna's father bought were beautiful, but they had never seen a plough before, let alone pulled one.

Getting the horses hitched to the plough was a daily disaster for Edna's father and brothers. The little girls thought it was as exciting as a Wild West show and insisted on watching. One mare, a deadly kicker, walked around the yard on her hind legs. Another two bolted whenever possible. The fourth one stomped and squealed and often lay stubbornly down on the ground. Charles Jaques was usually close to tears as he cursed the mustangs and tried to back them up to the plough. The procedure was so dangerous that he would not let Edna and her sisters stay and watch unless they sat on the low sloping roof of the barn.

After the horses were finally hitched to the plough, the show continued. The mustangs had only two speeds: "run" and "refuse to move." Once they started to pull, they tore along the fields with Edna's father riding the plough, howling and clumsily waving a whip in the air. The boys ran alongside with the reins in their hands, and the girls tore along behind determined not to miss any of the action. Whenever the mustangs were brought to a halt, there was a good chance they would lie down and refuse to budge.

Eventually Charles Jaques traded the two wildest of the mustangs to a rancher for a quiet, steady, well-broken pair. The new team knew more about ploughing than he did. They knew when to turn and, when placed at the front, hauled the remaining two mustangs along with them. Everyone was relieved, including the two bay mares, who once again ran wild in the foothills.

The Jaqueses managed to plough sixteen hectares that first year. Many of the ploughed rows were crooked, but they brought in a wonderful harvest of wheat and oats. The soil, which had never been farmed before, was rich, and although the Jaqueses did not realize it, they were farming in the bountiful "wet years". There would be no such bountiful harvests in the 1930s.

WATER PROBLEMS

The Jaques family left a home on the Great Lakes to homestead in an area where finding water was a constant problem. Homesteaders dug wells, but not always successfully. When Edna's older brother Bruce set up his own homestead, he dug thirteen wells, but never managed to locate a good one. Like most farmers in the area, Edna's father scraped out a pond to provide

14.2 Blue Monday in Manitoba. On wash day, Edna and the other women heated water in a boiler on the coal stove. The boiling water was then poured into the hand-cranked washing "machine". Excess water was removed from the heavy, wet clothes and sheets by pushing them through a hand-cranked wringer.

washing and drinking water for the house and livestock. The well water was hard and curdled the soap. Pond water was soft, but full of "wrigglers."

Without running water or electricity, the dreaded task of washing the clothes required time and hard physical labour. The day before washday, the precious water was hauled out of the pond and poured into a barrel that was dragged to the house. Edna's mother poured in lye and the next morning the water would be clear.

The water then had to be heated and every item scrubbed individually. Then everything had to be rinsed, wrung out by hand and hung to dry. By the end of washday, the Jaques women always had aching backs and hands that were rough and raw from scrubbing and wringing. That evening Edna's mother usually soaked her tired feet in a pan of hot water and Epsom Salts.

14.3 Blue Monday in Alberta. During wash day, women's arms and wrists became sore from rubbing, wringing and lifting heavy, water-soaked clothes.

14.4 Blue Monday in Alberta. After the wash, heavy tubs full of wet clothes, sheets and tablecloths were lugged outside. Edna, like other women, used wooden clothes pegs to hang them on long clothesline.

ALL ROADS LEAD TO BRIERCREST

Since the Jaqueses were the first settlers in the area, all new homesteaders stopped at Briercrest, the only house in the vast prairie landscape. As more and more settlers arrived, Briercrest became the centre of the growing settlement and all roads and trails passed through the Jaques yard.

Settlers came from places such as Ontario, England, Dakota, Montana and Missouri. The Jaqueses were lonely for neighbours and welcomed them all. Edna later wrote there was always company in their home. Some homesteaders arrived half eaten alive by the terrible clouds of mosquitoes and stinging flies along the trail.

Once the area was settled, there were still unexpected house guests. Sometimes parents rushing to visit the closest doctor dropped their children off at Briercrest. It might be a few days or even a few weeks before they returned to pick them up. Sometimes an only child on a homestead, lonely for company, would be dropped off to spend time with the Jaques children. All were warmly received by Edna's mother, who was an open-hearted and generous woman.

Edna later called these years "the gentle years," for the rains still fell, the crops were good and the vast, fenceless prairies still teemed with life. There were badgers, coyotes, deer, foxes, gophers, wild ducks and, in the autumn, Canada geese. There were also prairie chickens in the thousands. The Jaques boys could shoot this tasty wild bird from the kitchen door.

There was plenty of hard work, but their efforts produced plenty of food. As Edna's mother loved to cook and loved to watch others enjoy her cooking, the meals were large and delicious. In spite of all the good food, Edna remained petite, never growing over five feet (150 centimetres) in height even though her parents were much taller.

THE "FLASH"

Edna began writing poetry at the age of seven. She could be anywhere, doing anything, when, like a soft singing echo, words would form together in her mind. When she wrote the words down on scraps of paper, they took the shape of poems. Edna called this the "flash." She was afraid she would be laughed at, however, and hid her poems away.

By the age of fourteen, Edna was secretly writing poetry every day. One day, her brother Clyde crept up on her and snatched the paper out of her hand. He liked her poem although at first he refused to believe his little sister had written it. Later that summer he offered to take some of her poetry to the *Moose Jaw Times*. At that time, newspapers were the only reading material for many families, and newspapers often bought and printed poetry. The owner of the *Times* was impressed with Edna's talent and bought her three poems on the spot.

A rail line came through the area around 1911 and Edna's world was no longer limited to the few settler families around Briercrest. The area was now flooded with new businesses and tradesmen. Young men far outnumbered young women, and twenty-year-old Edna and her sisters had a wonderful social life, full of parties and dances.

Edna continued to write her poetry, however. By now she was writing a poem a week for the *Moose Jaw Times* and two a month for the *Saskatchewan Farmer* magazine. She received $1.50 for each poem that was printed. For the next thirty years, Edna had a poem published in every issue of the *Saskatchewan Farmer*, always for the same price of $1.50 a poem. She also agreed to write a poem a day for the *Winnipeg Free Press*. Edna still wanted time to spend with all the other young people in the area, however, so she stopped writing a daily poem for the *Free Press* after seven months. During her life, Edna wrote over 3000 poems, filling fifty-six fat scribblers with them. Her poems often celebrated the everyday things of her life.

"IN FLANDERS NOW"

In her twenties Edna decided to see more of the world by working her way to the west coast. In Calgary she worked in the sewing room of a hospital. Edna loved and memorized the famous poem "In Flanders Fields," written by a Canadian military doctor named John McCrae. One day in the hospital sewing room, Edna had the flash. She searched frantically for paper. Finding none, she turned over a box that held spools of thread, and hastily scribbled a poem she called "In Flanders Now" on the bottom of the box. Edna's poem was an answer to John McCrae's challenge: "To you from failing hands we throw / The torch; be yours to hold it high." Her poem, "In Flanders Now" was one Canadian poet speaking to another.

The *Calgary Herald* printed "In Flanders Now" and the poem was quickly picked up and reprinted in hundreds of American newspapers. The Everywoman's Clubs in the United States reprinted it in a little folder that they sold to raise funds to restore a library in Brussels. The organization raised over a million dollars by selling copies of the poem; Edna Jaques made forty dollars.

Edna then travelled on to Vancouver where she was one of fourteen women who worked on a passenger ship cleaning the cabins and waiting on tables. After a year of that, she went to business college and then worked at the *Vancouver Province*. For the next twenty years that newspaper printed ten of Edna's poems every month.

Edna, however, missed her family. She returned to Saskatchewan, and there she bumped into Ernest Jamieson, an old boyfriend everyone called Jimmy. They married in Moose Jaw in November 1921. The marriage was a disaster.

14.5 While homesteading with her husband and daughter, Edna became homesick for the broad prairie horizons.

HOMESTEAD HORRORS

Likable Jimmy, who came from a good Ontario family, was pleasant and made friends easily. However, he was lazy. When Jimmy lost his leather goods business a few years later, he decided they should homestead in the north where there was still available land. Their new homestead, almost sixty-five kilometres west of Prince Albert, Saskatchewan, was covered with tamarack and poplar trees. Edna cried when she first saw the desolate wooden shack that was to be home to Jimmy, herself and their baby, Joyce, for the next four years. The bedroom did not even have a wooden floor, so the bed rested on the dirt. Mice ran across the beds and their faces as they slept. In the summer they were plagued by black flies, mosquitoes and flying ants.

There was no well on the homestead, and Edna had to haul water from the muskeg covering part of their land. She tied little Joyce to a tree, ran to get the water, lugged the heavy bucket back to the tree and then untied her. Joyce then toddled back home behind her mother.

Edna was used to hardship, but this was different. Her parents had worked as a team to carve a living out of the land. Jimmy simply wandered off by himself for a week or so at a time, without explanation, leaving Edna and the baby to fend for themselves. There was not even a door on the cabin until October of that first year. Edna's closest neighbours worried about her and finally put a door on the cabin themselves.

In the four years they were there, Jimmy, who was fond of sleeping until noon, never did get around to putting a roof on their crude log barn. There were no fences, pens or food for their livestock. The first winter, timber wolves howled at night as they hunted in the muskeg. It was bitterly cold, and Edna had to spend much of her time cutting wood to burn in the shack's stove. By spring, out of all the livestock, only one cow, one horse and one chicken had survived. The others had starved to death or been killed by the wolves. Edna, Jimmy and Joyce lived on porridge, dry bread, beans and pancakes.

When Edna was a child, her mother had been homesick for trees. Once a year the Jaques family had seen a few trees when they went to a First of July picnic at "old Buchanan's ranch." Almost in tears, Edna's mother had lovingly patted them. Now, as an adult on her own homestead, Edna was homesick for the prairies. She felt walled in by the tamaracks and poplars, and longed for the clean sweep of a prairie horizon.

ESCAPE

Although Edna was only in her mid-thirties, her hard homestead life aged her prematurely: she was haggard and her hair was almost white. Her parents, concerned about her health, sent her a train ticket in the fall of the fourth year and invited her to spend the winter with them in Victoria, British Columbia, where they had rented a little cottage. Crazy with joy at the chance to escape, Edna and Joyce left the homestead never to return.

They spent a wonderful winter with Edna's parents in the mild climate of beautiful Victoria. Later, Jimmy visited them for a week. When he left, he told Edna they were breaking up and that Edna had a better chance of looking after Joyce than he did. They shook hands and never saw each other again.

Edna's parents returned to the prairies in the spring and Edna, who had only $9.65 to her name when Jimmy left, supported herself and her child by working for a year as maid and waitress in a small west coast hotel.

She then returned with Joyce to Briercrest, which her parents had sold to her brother Clyde in 1929. By this time the nine-year drought that devastated the prairies during the "Dirty Thirties" had set in and there were hardly any crops. Clyde, now married with five children of his own, had nonetheless invited Edna to stay with them that winter saying, "We'll all starve together."

THE DIRTY THIRTIES

The economy had boomed in the 1920s after World War I. By the end of the decade, however, industries in Canada and around the world were producing more goods than people could buy. Investors became nervous at the slump in sales, and rather than buy more shares in companies, they began to sell off the shares they owned. As more and more investors sold, the panic spread. In October 1929 share prices plunged and the stock market collapsed. Many people who had invested their savings in the stock market lost everything. Many others lost their jobs as the economy crumbled and businesses closed.

The Great Depression began. In Canada's midwest, farmers struggled with both the poor economy and with the drought and plagues of insects that devastated their crops.

Saskatchewan was especially hard hit. In the boom years of 1928-29, the average income per person in Canada was $471 per year, while in Saskatchewan it was $478. By 1933, the average income in Canada had dropped to $247 per year, but in Saskatchewan it had plunged to a mere $135.

In the hot, dry summers of the 1930s, the wind carried away the rich prairie topsoil no longer held in place by the prairie wool. Many families watched their farms blow away, leaving only a wasteland behind. There was so much blowing soil that the railways used snow ploughs to push drifts of it up to three metres high off the tracks. It was indeed the "Dirty Thirties."

Edna and the others fought a losing battle against the plagues of army worms that relentlessly swarmed into the drought-stricken area and covered the roads, sidewalks, fields and fences with a heaving, squirming mass of green. Over 66 000 people left Saskatchewan between 1931 and 1937, as exhausted families, defeated by the insects and the drought, simply abandoned their farms.

Hundreds of prairie children growing up in that nine-year-long drought did not even recognize rain. Edna's five-year-old niece once ran into the house in a state of terror. She was frightened because "water was coming out of the sky."

When the Briercrest pond dried up, Edna's brothers, Bruce and Clyde, could not stand to watch their horses slowly die of thirst. One terrible morning they shot all twenty-seven of them, one by one. When the job was done, the men cried as if their hearts were breaking.

NEW DOORS OPEN

In spite of the hard times, Edna continued writing and selling poetry. One day, the flash came to her when she was surrounded by turmoil and unhappiness. She wrote the poem "Thankful for What," which celebrates the little things in life. *Good Housekeeping* magazine printed it in their November 1932 issue, and newspapers quickly reprinted it until it reached a million homes. The *New York Times* chose it as the outstanding poem of the year. Once again, Edna received all of forty dollars for the poem.

Another time the flash came one evening as Edna watched her brother Bruce carrying a lantern in his barn. She rushed into the house and scribbled the poem "Man With A Lantern" on the cover of a writing pad.

Edna was thrilled when two booklets of her poems, entitled *Wide Horizons* and *Drifting Soil* were published in 1932. In 1935, her first book

14.6 Edna admired the strength and courage of the women who lived through the long prairie drought. Here, an Alberta farm woman and her daughter dig up potatoes in the earlier "wet year".

of poetry, entitled *My Kitchen Window*, was published. Edna's dearest friend, writer and suffragist Nellie McClung had persuaded a Toronto company to publish the book. *My Kitchen Window* was a success, and later collections of Edna's poems include *Dreams in Your Heart, Beside Still Waters, Roses in December, Aunt Hattie's Place, Back Door Neighbors, Hills of Home, Fireside Poems, Golden Road,* and *Prairie Born.*

Edna's poems were read and loved by many, but they did not bring in much money. She always had to work at other jobs in order to provide a living for herself and Joyce. She received a great deal of fan mail, but often had to wait until payday to buy stamps for her replies.

Once during the Great Depression, Edna was the guest speaker at the Women's Canadian Club in Moose Jaw. She was a success and eventually travelled back and forth across Canada on speaking engagements. Her poetry was so well known that she was welcomed everywhere she went. Once, after giving a speech in Victoria, she met and shook the hand of artist Emily Carr. Emily wanted Edna to shake her dog's paw too, and Edna did.

In 1935, Edna persuaded the publicity department of the Canadian Pacific Railway to give her a pass for the prairie provinces. It was at the height of the drought and the Great Depression, and she spoke at many of the lonely little towns and villages along the rail line—places that could not afford to pay her train fare but were delighted by a visit from the poet Edna Jaques.

Edna was moved by the uncomplaining courage of the people she spoke to in the drought-stricken areas of Saskatchewan and Alberta. She admired the hard-working women who had not bought clothing for themselves in five years and for whom a jar of pickles was the only Christmas treat. Edna described them as "valiant women, as brave as any soldier on any battlefield."

WORLD WAR II

During World War II, Edna worked in a munitions factory near Toronto, Ontario, building the tools of war. She then worked in Ottawa as a secretary and later as a news writer for the War Prices and Trade Board. At one point, she travelled on her own to Alaska to write about the building of the Alaska Highway, and her article later appeared in *Macleans* magazine. Throughout the war, she received fan mail from homesick soldiers, who read her poetry at their posts overseas.

After the war, Edna returned to Toronto. Her daughter Joyce, who had worked as a nurse and then as an airline stewardess, married a successful businessman in 1945. Edna lived in Toronto with her daughter, son-in-law, and four grandchildren for the rest of her life.

LATER YEARS

Edna's poems continued to delight her many admirers. In 1952, a national opinion poll picked her as one of Canada's most popular women. In 1976 Edna was named Woman of the Year by the premier of Ontario. Edna's excellent autobiography, *Uphill All the Way*, was published in 1977. The book is a moving account of this extraordinary woman and her extraordinary life.

By the time Edna Jaques, Canada's "Poet Laureate of the home," died in 1978, her poetry had touched millions with its warmth and gentle wisdom.

Further suggested reading:

Jaques, Edna. *Uphill All the Way*. Saskatoon: Western Producer Prairie
    Books, 1977.

15.1 Some members of Newfoundland's "leisure class" that Margaret Duley was born into

CHAPTER 15

AUTHOR

MARGARET DULEY
—————— (1894 - 1968) ——————

I have left them a heritage. In their library will be a little corner of Margaret Duley's works.

— Margaret Duley

Margaret chatted with the other dinner guests at Government House as they waited for the next course to be served. At the head of the elegant table sat their host, the Englishman appointed by Britain to be Governor of Newfoundland.

A maid brought a serving dish of steaming hot turnip into the dining room. The Governor raised his eyebrows and pointed at the dish. "Home in England," he sneered, "we do not eat turnip. We feed it to the cattle!"

Margaret flushed with anger at the insult to Newfoundland. "Care for some, your Excellency?" she quickly asked with a smile.

EARLY LIFE

Margaret Iris Duley was born on 27 September 1894, in St. John's, the capital of Newfoundland. Her mother, Tryphena Soper Duley, had been raised as a member of Newfoundland's "leisure class," and her father, Thomas Duley, was an Englishman who owned a successful jewellery business in St. John's.

Although the Duleys lived in the city, they sometimes spent their summer holidays in the small Newfoundland seaport town of Carbonear. As a result, Margaret observed outport life at an early age and later wrote about these isolated villages and their inhabitants in her novels.

NEWFOUNDLAND'S ELITE

For much of Margaret's life, Newfoundland was a self-governing outpost of the British Empire. The city of St. John's controlled both the island's social and economic life. Newfoundland's high society consisted of upper class Protestants who were often the owners of old shipping and trading companies. Some wealthy and well-educated Roman Catholic families were also admitted into the charmed circle of St. John's elite.

The well-to-do often lived near Government House, which was home to the island's British governor. Government House carefully selected which young ladies of St. John's were to dance with the officers of the British ships that made courtesy calls at the port of St. John's.

Margaret's family home, complete with servants, was a comfortable one and she grew up in the company of the sons and daughters of St. John's elite. She loved to read and, when lessons became dull, often hid a book in her lap under her school desk. In 1910, she left school with the equivalent of a Grade 11 education. At that time, a university education was generally a privilege reserved for boys of wealthy families. Margaret had to find other ways to expand her mind.

ENGLAND

In 1911, Margaret made a trip to England to attend the wedding of her aunt. Margaret loved British history and literature and was proud of her English connections. Because of Newfoundland's strong ties with Britain, the children of well-to-do Newfoundlanders were often sent, not to Canada, but to the British Isles to further their education. Margaret, who admired the traditions and culture of England, went back in 1913 to study elocution at the London Academy of Music and Dramatic Art. While there, she developed the distinct English accent that she never lost.

When World War I broke out in Europe in 1914, Margaret returned to Newfoundland where she and her family were swept up in "the war effort."

WOMEN AND WORLD WAR I

When the war began, Newfoundland women were ready to assist. The fundraising talents of the island's middle- and upper-class women had supported churches, orphanages and public charities for many years. Now all women supported the war effort under the direction of the Women's Patriotic Association.

Newfoundland women raised funds to help train and equip the young men of the Newfoundland Regiment. The Women's Patriotic Association also co-ordinated thousands of female volunteers, in hundreds of locations across Newfoundland, to produce badly needed supplies for the soldiers.

When, in October of 1914, the British War Office appealed to "the women of the empire" to supply 300 000 pairs of grey socks for the troops, Newfoundland women rushed to help the men overseas. Margaret's mother recalled that women knitted socks at bridge parties, movie theatres, committee meetings and afternoon teas. Knitting parties became fashionable at all levels of society. Grey socks, especially the best way to shape heels and toes, the quality of the wool and the number of pairs already completed, became popular topics of conversation.

15.2 During World War I, the Women's Patriotic Association (WPA) of Newfoundland established 208 branches. By 1914, over 15000 WPA women were drawn into the work of raising funds and producing clothing for the soldiers overseas. After the war, women used the WPA network in the votes for women movement.

One Newfoundland soldier overseas wrote to a St. John's newspaper "A Newfoundland sock is the best in the world and is prized by every soldier." He boasted that soldiers from other regiments often asked to buy a pair of Newfoundland socks.

Never before had the traditional "women's work" of Newfoundland received such open approval. Prior to the war, it had generally been ignored or discounted as having no value to society. Public opinion regarding women and what they could accomplish, however, began to change during World War I. Newfoundland women such as Margaret produced, to the exacting standards of the British War Office, thousands of heavy mitts, scarves, wool helmets and thick day shirts for the soldiers who faced winter in the trenches of Europe. For the poor young men mangled by the Great War, women made pyjamas, pillows, pillow slips, blankets, bandages, and limb pillows.

One St. John's newspaper nicknamed the Women's Patriotic Association the "Army of Service." It is estimated that the women of Newfoundland had raised almost $500 000 in supplies and cash by the end of the war. In today's money, the total value of the contributions of the Women's Patriotic Association would amount to about $6.5 million. Newfoundland women had proved that "women's work" had financial worth.

THE HIGH PRICE OF WAR

As a result of outstanding bravery during the war, the Newfoundland Regiment was renamed the "Royal Newfoundland Regiment." By the end of the war, however, more than 4000 Newfoundlanders had been wounded or killed overseas. Based on population size, Newfoundland had one of the highest casualty rates of the British Empire. Almost an entire generation of Newfoundland males was destroyed in terrible battles such as the Gallipoli landings, Beaumont Hamel, the Somme, Passchendaele and Vimy Ridge.

Margaret's youngest brother was killed in 1918; her eldest brother was badly wounded. Her third brother suffered as well. He was declared unfit for service because he had tuberculosis, but he refused to explain to others why he had not joined the army. As a result, he was called a coward and malicious people sent him the white feathers of cowardice in the mail.

The love of Margaret's life was also a casualty of war. Dashing young Jack Clift was wounded in battle and won the Military Cross. However he survived the war and returned to study law in St. John's. Margaret was shattered when Jack died two years later of a kidney disease caused by his war experience. He was twenty-six when he died.

Newfoundland itself was burdened with a huge war debt. Then came the Great Depression of the 1930s. With no markets for its products and thousands of people out of work, Newfoundland could no longer pay the interest on its debts, and Britain had to step in. Margaret and other Newfoundlanders were upset when, in 1934, Britain set up a Commission Government that ended the island's self-government. Newfoundland was returned to colonial status until it joined Confederation in 1949.

LIFE GOES ON

A friend of Margaret's father proposed to her, but Margaret refused him, even though her parents pressed her to marry the respectable and well-regarded suitor.

Margaret's father died in 1920 and left a small estate that would give her and her sister each the yearly sum of $250. At that time it was enough money to allow Margaret, who lived at her mother's home, to continue moving in the "right" circles.

Margaret was frequently in demand, for she was attractive, witty, stimulating and fun to have around. Like other women of her social class, she played bridge, went to the theatre, attended dances and balls and was a frequent guest at Government House.

But this was not enough for such an intelligent woman. In order to stimulate her mind, Margaret read a great deal and became a member of the Ladies' Reading Room and the Current Events Club.

THE CURRENT EVENTS CLUB

In 1891, three years before Margaret's birth, Newfoundland women formally petitioned the legislature for the right to vote. Premier Whiteway, who believed a woman's main role was one of "adornment," opposed women's suffrage. He claimed that it was woman's "province to exercise her influence in the home circle ... and to meet her husband with a kindly greeting when he returned from his daily occupation." For some reason he seemed to believe that being able to vote meant that a woman would be "absent from the household." The first request for the right to vote was turned down, but women known as suffragists kept the dream of women's suffrage alive.

Around 1909, women who had often attended lectures at a particular men's club were banned from future lectures after they spoke out in favour of women's rights. Annoyed suffragists immediately formed a women's social, political and educational club in St. John's called The Ladies Reading Room. Within a few weeks the group had 125 members. The Current Events Club, which met on Saturdays, was the political branch of the Ladies Reading Room. Here women members gave papers, discussed and analyzed issues, and developed public-speaking skills. They listened to stimulating papers on many topics, but often the papers discussed women's rights. Many influential women in St. John's became suffragists after taking part in the lively discussions of the Current Events Club.

When World War I began, they generally put aside their suffrage work and focused on the war effort. The Women's Patriotic Association, with its wonderful network of hard-working women, had many suffragists in leadership positions. After the war the suffragists put this network to good use in the Votes for Women campaign.

VOTES FOR WOMEN

Proud of the public service role they had played during the war, women wanted to continue to contribute during the peace. Much-needed social reform affecting women and children would not happen, suffragists believed, until they had the right to vote and the right to run for office. It was time for women to have the vote, they argued, because of their rights as human beings ("natural rights"), because of their unique, caring roles as mothers ("maternal rights") and because of the importance and economic value of traditional "women's work," demonstrated by the outstanding financial contributions they made during World War I.

In early 1920, Margaret and other suffragists formed the Women's Franchise League. The most active members, such as Margaret's mother, were often the married, middle-aged St. John's elite. They had the time, money and organizational skills to work on the Votes for Women campaign. Younger members, like Margaret, were often daughters of suffragists or professionals such as nurses or school principals. Membership in the Women's Franchise League crossed religious lines and included active members from Roman Catholic and Protestant denominations.

When suffragists such as Margaret looked for support in their cause, they found that some of the powerful men of their own economic class were hostile. One woman recalled enraged men ordering suffragists from their offices. Another spent a great deal of time and effort collecting signatures on a women's suffrage petition, only to have her clergyman father deliberately burn it behind her back.

By 1925, Newfoundland suffragists had collected 20 000 signatures on petitions supporting women's suffrage. Newfoundland and South Africa were by now the only British dominions where women did not have the vote. With courage and determination, however, Margaret and others continued gathering support, and in March 1925, the Suffrage Bill was passed. Newfoundland women finally had the vote even if they did not have equality: men could vote at age 21, but women could not vote until age 25.

THE EYES OF THE GULL

In 1928, Margaret took a boat trip with her brother up the coast of Labrador. During that trip, a gull briefly hovered in front of her. Its eyes were like "yellow ice" and she saw them as a "symbol of the piteous heart of the north." When Margaret wrote her first book in the early 1930s, she used that fierce, yellow-eyed image in the title and throughout the novel. Margaret, who had never written before, simply plunged into novel writing. *The Eyes of the Gull* tells the story of a thirty-year-old woman who seeks freedom from her bleak outport life and domineering mother. The young woman rebels against a life cramped by the rules governing women's lives. The novel, full of memorable characters and grim humour, does not romanticize Newfoundland's outport life. Part of Margaret was drawn to the outports, but part of her was angered by the poverty and repelled by the savage winds and heaving seas. Published in Britain in 1936, *The Eyes of the Gull* received good reviews in Britain, but Margaret's acquaintances in St. John's were unimpressed.

TWO MORE NOVELS

Each of Margaret's first three novels give readers a penetrating, sometimes stark view of a woman's life in Newfoundland. Margaret's second novel, Cold Pastoral, may have been influenced by the true story of a young girl who was lost in the woods in 1936. In this novel, a lost, thirteen-year-old

15.3 Margaret's novels often give insights into the character of the Newfoundland people. Above, farm work in Pleasantville, Newfoundland, 1895.

15.4 Quidi Vidi Village, Newfoundland. Most of Margaret's novels were set in the outports of Newfoundland.

outport girl is eventually adopted and raised by one of St. John's elite families. The book was published in London, England, possibly in 1939. Margaret's publishing company was bombed during World War II, and all its records were destroyed, so she probably did not make any money from her second novel.

Highway to Valour was Margaret's third published novel. A young outport girl, gifted with healing powers, is orphaned by a tidal wave that sweeps her family home out to sea. The young orphan becomes the governess in an upper-class family and must decide what to do with the rest of her life.

15.5 One of Newfoundland's outport women. Margaret admired the hard-working women of Newfoundland's outports. In Cold Pastoral, she includes the fisherman Benedict and his wife Josephine as characters. "In Benedict's world," Margaret wrote, "a woman could make or break a man. Had he been bound to a slattern the toil of her hands would have been for naught. Josephine made him!"

Margaret's novels often portray the wild storms of Newfoundland so vividly that the weather almost becomes a character. Such a tidal wave actually occurred in Newfoundland in 1929, killing twenty-seven people.

Highway to Valour, which was published in New York in 1941, is generally viewed as Margaret's best novel. The *Globe and Mail* praised it as "an exceptional picture of Newfoundland and Labrador," and the *New York Times* talked of Margaret's "word gift."

LAST NOVEL

Margaret's last published novel, *Novelty on Earth*, came out in New York in 1942 and in Britain in 1944 (retitled *Green Afternoon*). It was also published in a Swedish translation in 1946 (retitled *How Sara Struggled*). Unlike Margaret's other novels, *Novelty on Earth* was set in what could be any British colony in the summer, and then in London in the autumn.

As Margaret grew older, she made fun of the social pursuits of her own elite group. Trips to Government House often bored her, but they did provide her with material for her books. Margaret questions the social and moral codes of the times through *Novelty on Earth*'s story of a woman's unhappy love affair. This book received many favourable reviews.

Margaret's fifth novel was rejected by her publisher and the manuscript has disappeared. Little is known about this work, for Margaret was always secretive about her writing. Even her friends often did not know what she was working on until her next novel appeared in print.

WORLD WAR II

Margaret's last book, *The Caribou Hut*, is a lively account of how the city of St. John's coped with the enormous influx of Canadian and American servicemen (16 000 by 1946) during World War II. Servicemen spent their spare time drinking and brawling until a hostel, named the Caribou Hut, was created to give them a place to spend their off hours. Margaret did volunteer work at the Caribou Hut and probably wrote her non-fiction account, which was published in 1949, without payment.

The Women's Patriotic Association of Newfoundland sprang back to life during the war. Margaret worked as a stock keeper for the Women's Patriotic Association, sorting and packing thousands of hand-knitted garments for the soldiers fighting in Europe. She also worked with the St. John's Ambulance Corps.

LOVE AND HATE

Margaret dedicated her novel *Highway to Valour* to Newfoundland, which, she wrote, is "a country which the author loves and hates." An intelligent and perceptive woman, Margaret realized that her life was full of contradictions. She disliked the harsh conditions of outport life, yet felt compelled to examine and explain it to the outside world. She often made fun of the elite St. John's group to which she belonged, but she did not try to leave its circle. Margaret loved England and called the boat that travelled between England and Newfoundland every two weeks, the "Home Boat," but she hated the Commission Government that Britain had set up. She enjoyed Newfoundland's ties to British monarchy, but was quick to point out the defects of British policy in Newfoundland. In *Highway to Valour*, Margaret's main character muses "They say the Englishman governs like the cock who thinks the sun rises to hear him crow."

AFTER THE WAR

After World War II, Margaret often visited her sister in North Carolina, as well as friends in New York and Montreal. From 1950 to 1952 she was the Public Relations Officer for the Red Cross and wrote newspaper articles as well as newsletters that were sent around the world. As part of her job, Margaret interviewed over two hundred people and wrote scripts for broadcast talks that were used on Radio Station CJON. Still interested in women's rights, she included talks on interesting women such as Florence Nightingale, founder of modern nursing, the famous singer Jenny Lind and Clara Barton, first president of the American Red Cross.

In 1952 Margaret went to England where she taped four short talks on the coronation of Queen Elizabeth II. The programs were broadcast on the popular British Broadcasting Corporation radio program "Calling from Britain to Newfoundland." She then travelled through France, Switzerland, Monaco and Italy. When she returned to England she prepared and read another script for the BBC. Her topic was the terrible fire that raged through St. John's in 1892. The BBC staff praised her script and her "distinguished" voice, and invited Margaret to give another talk any time she was in London.

THE END

Margaret returned to St. John's and was forced to face the fact that she was in financial difficulty. She took in boarders at her family home, but the building, which had been badly damaged by Margaret's previous tenant, required many costly repairs.

By 1955, Margaret 's health was beginning to decline. She had Parkinson's Disease, a nerve disorder with the early symptom of trembling limbs. In 1956, her friends noticed that Margaret inched her playing cards across the table during a game so that the tremble in her hands would be less noticeable.

Parkinson's Disease does not affect mental ability, but as it progresses it causes constant head shaking, an unblinking, rigid facial expression, a stooped, rigid posture and a stiff, unbalanced, shuffling walk. By 1959, Margaret's right hand was so crippled she could no longer write letters and she had difficulty running her home. There is no known cure for Parkinson's, and the disease finally forced Margaret, who had always valued her independence and freedom, to give up her home. She moved in with her devoted sister-in-law and niece who cared for her for a number of years. Margaret died at the age of 73.

HERITAGE

Margaret Iris Duley was an accomplished writer who truthfully recorded the sights and sounds of her native land. Critics rate her as one of Newfoundland's finest writers for her skilful, unflinching portrayal of life in the outports. Although she is often neglected as a writer, the novels of Margaret Duley are a heritage that Canadians can still treasure and enjoy.

Further suggested reading:

Feder, Alison. *Margaret Duley: Newfoundland Novelist, a Biographical and Critical Study*. St. John's: Harry Cuff Publications Limited, 1983.

Duley, Margot I. *Where Once Our Mothers Stood We Stand /Women's Suffrage in Newfoundland 1890 - 1925*. Charlottetown: gynergy books, 1993.

CHAPTER 16

ARTIST

PITSEOLAK
—— (1904 - 1983) ——

I draw the things I have never seen, the monsters and spirits, and I draw the old ways, the things we did long ago before there were many white men.

— Pitseolak

Pitseolak left the Co-op building clutching the money which Saumik, the Left-Handed One, had given her for her first drawings. She had felt nervous when she showed her work to Saumik, but he had liked her three drawings. He had even asked her to make more!

Pitseolak looked down at the money in her hand. Was there enough to buy a few things for her grandchildren? She counted the money and stopped in amazement. There was more money here than she would be paid for making an entire parka, which took much skill and effort.

"Saumik must have made a mistake when he gave me twenty dollars," Pitseolak thought."It is too much!"

A HAPPY CHILDHOOD

Pitseolak was born in 1904 on Nottingham Island, in Hudson Strait, in Canada's Eastern Arctic. Her people were the Inuit, whom other Canadians called "Eskimos" at that time. Inuit, which means "the people," has always been their own word for themselves, and today it is used throughout Canada.

Pitseolak's mother and father (Timangiak and Ottochie) and her three brothers were on a long and dangerous journey at the time of Pitseolak's birth. The family had left northern Quebec and were rowing a sealskin umiak, or large, open boat, across Hudson Strait to join relatives on Baffin Island.

Pitseolak's family lived in "the old way," and her childhood was a happy one. Her father hunted with bow and arrow or spear and the family often moved to different camps on Baffin Island, for there were no permanent homes. Even on the coldest winter days Pitseolak and her brothers and sister left their snow house (igloo) or their insulated tent-hut (kaamuk) and played make-believe games outside with their toy sleds and

16.1 The artist Pitseolak, as she appeared on a Canadian postal stamp. Stamp reproduced courtesy of Canada Post Corporation.

dolls. Every year, Pitseolak's mother made the large sealskin tent that was the family summer home.

THE OLD WAYS

Pitseolak's father died before she reached her teens, and that same year a marriage was arranged, as was the custom, between Pitseolak and a skilled young hunter named Ashoona. At first Pitseolak was shy and frightened of her husband-to-be, but he was a good provider and the marriage was a happy one. Life in the harsh Arctic climate was a struggle, however, and a woman needed to give birth to many children if she hoped to see even two or three of them survive. Pitseolak gave birth to seventeen children, but only five lived to adulthood. She found that giving birth was hard and was grateful that other women helped during childbirth.

For some years, Pitseolak and her husband followed the traditional way of life of their ancestors, for there was no need to live any other way. Like her mother before her, Pitseolak made the family's summer tent and the waterproof "shell" of the kayaks and umiaks out of sealskin sewn together with sinew from caribou. Ashoona was an excellent hunter and brought Pitseolak high-quality furs, as well as caribou and seal skins that she made into clothing and other items for their growing family. They moved camp as often as ten times a year, in summer or in winter, in search of caribou and other game.

Although Pitseolak was content to live and raise her children in the Inuit traditional ways, the times were changing.

WINDS OF CHANGE

A Hudson's Bay Company trading post was built in Cape Dorset, Baffin Island, and before long Pitseolak's family no longer depended entirely on the hunt. They began making three trips a year to the Hudson's Bay post, often by dog sled. There, Ashoona traded fox skins for "white man's food" or "grub." The family bought items such as tea, molasses, shortening, baking powder, white wheat flour and salt. When there was a large demand for furs in Europe, they received many supplies in exchange for the white fox furs. When the trapping was poor, however, or whenever furs fell out of fashion, it was difficult for the Inuit to buy the imported goods the traders encouraged them to depend on for survival.

Pitseolak no longer made the family's summer tent out of sealskins. Instead, she made it out of canvas that the family bought at the trading post. Many Inuit families no longer used the skin boats that they had once made themselves. Instead, they bought and used wooden boats. The Inuit selected and used these and other "imported" items, such as tools and weapons, that fitted into their lifestyle. Some other imports, however, nearly destroyed them as a people.

The Inuit did not have any natural immunity to the many diseases that the outsiders had brought in, but were unable to cure. Tuberculosis, the deadly lung disease, spread through the Arctic, killing many. Wave after wave of epidemics—whooping cough, scarlet fever, influenza, measles—also swept through various Inuit communities in the Canadian Arctic. Thousands died, and Pitseolak's husband was one of them. During an epidemic in the late 1940s, Ashoona, the healthy and accomplished hunter, suddenly took sick and died within a few days.

16.2 Women like Pitseolak always used the warmest and best furs to make clothes for their children. Inuit children, such as the girl above, played outside in even extremely cold weather; sometimes the ends of their sleeves were sewn together so that their hands would not freeze.

HARDSHIP AND HUNGER

Pitseolak was now a widow responsible for raising her young family alone. The family deeply mourned his loss. One of the youngest sons, too young to understand, continued to search for his father whenever a dog team came into the camp.

There were other problems for the family as well. The eldest children were still teenagers at the time of Ashoona's death, and not yet experienced hunters. Without Ashoona to provide for them, the family struggled to survive. They lived in camps near Cape Dorset with other families. Although others helped, sometimes there was not even seal oil for the soapstone lamp (kudlik). The kudlik was the most important item in the igloo, for it was usually the only source of heat and light. It was used to cook bannock (a type of bread), warm up water and dry out clothes.

There was hardship and hunger in the lean years that followed Ashoona's death until Pitseolak's sons became good hunters and provided the needed skins and food.

FROM SOUVENIR TO ART

By the early 1950s the Inuit were facing terrible problems. Many no longer lived on the traditional foods they had once hunted on land and sea. Instead, they became more and more dependent on the imported foods they obtained through the fur trade. The white people's "grub" they were able to buy was not nutritious and many Inuit began to suffer from malnutrition. Their average life expectancy was thirty-four years, many children died at an early age, and the Inuit population was shrinking.

Traditionally, the Inuit had carefully crafted the practical objects they used on a daily basis. They did not, however, produce "art for art's sake" and did not have a word for "art" in their language. A group that moves frequently in search of food, cannot be weighed down with art objects that do not have a practical use. But their everyday objects such as utensils, toys and weapons were often beautifully carved out of bone, ivory or antler. Soapstone, the material we now associate with Inuit sculpture, was generally only used to carve seal-oil lamps.

In the 1800s, the Inuit sold small ivory carvings to the crews of whaling ships, but the objects were considered souvenirs, not art. By the 1950s however, the art world was beginning to look with new interest at objects created by the native inhabitants of Africa, South America and the South Pacific. The objects they created were now viewed as "art," and valued as such.

In the late 1940s a man by the name of Jim Houston was impressed by the Inuit carvings he saw while he was on a sketching trip in the Arctic. The Inuit called him "Saumik," meaning "Left-Handed One." Houston took back samples to the Canadian Guild of Crafts and encouraged the Inuit to create more. He returned to the Arctic, first on behalf of the Guild and later as an officer of the Canadian government, and took more carvings back to sell in the south. The art world was impressed with the carvings, and suddenly there were many willing buyers of Inuit sculpture. By 1951, the Guild had sold over eleven thousand pieces of Inuit art.

THE CO-OPS

The sale of Inuit carvings began to bring much-needed cash to the Inuit. During the 1940s, the Canadian government had encouraged the Inuit to live in bungalows in permanent settlements along the Arctic coastline. In that way, fuel and food could be brought in by ship during the Arctic summers, and education and health care provided. It was, however, a traumatic change for the Inuit. Once a self-sufficient people who survived by moving from site to site in search of game, many Inuit now remained in one place and survived on purchased items. The Inuit now had to find a way to "make a living" in order to purchase items.

In the 1950s, Jim Houston became the Northern Affairs administrator for the Cape Dorset region on the west side of Baffin Island. While in Cape Dorset, Houston founded the first Inuit-owned art co-operative in the Northwest Territories. The co-operative gave the Cape Dorset Inuit a way to make and market their own art, while sharing the profits among co-op members. The choice of the co-operative as a business vehicle was a natural one for a people such as the Inuit, whose culture insisted upon sharing in good times and in bad.

The founding of the West Baffin Eskimo Cooperative brought new money to the Cape Dorset community and freed the Inuit from total reliance on the ups and downs of the fur trade. The co-op also changed the life of Pitseolak.

THE FIRST DRAWINGS

When Pitseolak moved into the permanent settlement at Cape Dorset, she made money by taking part in a sewing project begun by Alma Houston. Pitseolak began sewing and selling parkas and other garments, but this work was hard and did not produce much income. She heard that others in Cape Dorset were earning money by drawing on paper. Jim Houston believed that the Cape Dorset Inuit had the talent to produce and sell graphic art and he encouraged them to draw by purchasing much of their finished work.

Pitseolak, who was now fifty-four years of age, bought a few pieces of paper and drew some pictures. It was the first time that she had ever drawn on paper, for in the Arctic, paper was a fragile substance that was useless in the traditional Inuit way of life. However, one of Pitseolak's daughters-in-law had died, and she was caring for two young grandchildren. Piseolak hoped her drawings would earn enough money to purchase items for them.

Jim Houston recognized Pitseolak's talent, paid her for those first drawings, and encouraged her to bring him more. From that beginning, Pitseolak became a serious graphic artist, devoting many hours to her new career. Sometimes this talented woman drew as many as six pictures in one morning. In all, Pitseolak produced over seven thousand drawings; some two hundred of them were made into fine art prints by the West Baffin Eskimo Cooperative. As a result of her talent, her persistence and her hard work, Pitseolak became one of the most famous of the famous Cape Dorset artists.

16.3 Over 300 years ago, European traders introduced beads, cotton thread and steel needles as trade items. Inuit women began to use their creative talents to produce beautiful, intricate beadwork designs on their clothing. Here, Inuit women display their beaded artiggi (inner fur garment) in 1903/1904.

GRAPHIC ART IN A PAPERLESS SOCIETY

At first it seems amazing that Pitseolak, who lived in a paperless society until her fifties, could become one of Canada's best-known graphic artists. Inuit women, however, were traditionally skilled in various types of graphic art. For hundreds, possibly thousands of years, body-decoration (tattooing) was a form of graphic art which young Inuit women used to beautify themselves and to prepare themselves for the pain of childbirth. Caribou sinew was soaked in the oil and soot of the seal-oil lamp, then pulled by a needle through the face, shoulder or arm skin to form various designs. Once the swelling went away, permanent black marks were left in the skin. Pitseolak's mother had tattoo marks on her face, and Pitseolak had a few on her arm.

Inuit women also traditionally put their creative talent to work by decorating their clothing with fringes and with different colours of fur. After European traders started bringing in beads and steel needles, the women began to decorate garments with elaborate beadwork and bead fringes.

Like other Inuit women, Pitseolak had used her traditional skills to embroider animal designs on the garments she made. She had also used different coloured skins to inlay traditional patterns and designs on the parkas she created.

16.4 The beautiful clothing Inuit women produced was "wearable art". Inuit women also expressed their creativity by decorating their body with tattoos. Above, a woman in the paperless Inuit society of 1903/1904 displays her artistic talent.

All her life, Pitseolak had used her creative talents to beautify the clothing she produced. The decoration of clothing had been a natural outlet for her creative talent. At the age of fifty-four, Pitseolak then began to place creative shapes and designs on *paper*, rather than on textiles. It was a natural transfer of the graphic design skills she had mastered while living in "the old way." Although the art world may believe that Pitseolak's art career began when she placed shapes and forms on paper, it truly began when, years earlier, she had used her talent to decorate caribou and sealskin garments for her family.

SEA PIGEON

Traditional Inuit names did not indicate the gender or the status of a person. As well, surnames (last names) did not exist, and more than one person could have the same name. In the 1970s the government introduced "Project Surname," which encouraged the reluctant Inuit to use names of male family members as surnames. Project Surname was supposed to reduce confusion for the government, but instead it caused confusion. Sometimes Pitseolak used the first name of her father, Ottochie, as a surname and sometimes she used that of her husband, Ashoona. Although *Pitseolak*, the Inuit word for sea pigeon, is a fairly common name, Pitseolak is still widely known by her first name alone.

THE ART OF PITSEOLAK

Pitseolak's drawings have a highly personal and distinctive style about them. They are often lively, with a feeling of joy and humour, and they show a strong sense of balance and design. Pitseolak began by using black and brown ink in her drawings. Later, however, she started to include large blocks of vivid colour in her designs. Like the brightly coloured wildflowers that bloom in the Arctic summer, many of Pitseolak's drawings were filled with colour and life. From her rich imagination Pitseolak drew supernatural creatures from Inuit stories. From her memories of living on the land, she drew Arctic wildlife and "the old ways" which she and her children had lived and watched disappear. Much of her art portrayed the experiences of Inuit women.

SUCCESS

Demand for the graphics of Pitseolak and others in her settlement increased until Cape Dorset, a small Arctic community in the Northwest Territories, won international acclaim. Today most public art galleries of North America and Europe proudly carry at least one "Dorset graphic" in their collections.

Pitseolak became one of the most famous members of the artist's colony at Cape Dorset. From 1960 to 1984, her graphic designs were included in the annual Cape Dorset print collections. In 1971, *Pitseolak: Pictures Out of My Life*, a book of tape-recorded interviews containing over sixty of her drawings, was published. Later, the National Film Board of Canada made an animated documentary film

16.5 Pitseolak's drawing of a woman moving camp in summertime appears on a Canadian postal stamp. Pitseolak playfully exaggerates the size of the mosquitoes that appear during Arctic summers. Stamp reproduced courtesy of Canada Post Corporation.

Academy of the Arts. One year later she received a Canada Council Senior Arts grant, and the International Cinemedia Centre made two films about her art (*The Way We Live Today; Spirits and Monsters*). In 1977, Pitseolak received the Order of Canada in recognition of her important contribution to Canadian art. The Order of Canada is Canada's highest civilian honour.

THE POWER OF THE PEN

The money Pitseolak earned from her drawings allowed her to support herself and the many members of her family. Size and strength have nothing to do with artistic ability, and financial success suddenly made talented Inuit women such as Pitseolak powerful figures in their communities. The respect that was once reserved for strong male hunters now shifted to those who were skilled with the pen, which had become the new instrument for survival in the Arctic.

In spite of her financial success and her pride in her work, Pitseolak remained wise and warm, humorous and unselfish. She encouraged her daughter, Nawpachee (sometimes spelled Napachie, Nawpashee, Napatchie or Napassie), and her sons' wives to begin drawing. At her urging, her daughter and three of her daughters-in-law became established Cape Dorset graphic artists. The family Pitseolak headed was an artistic one, for three of Pitseolak's four sons became sculptors.

END OF A WAY OF LIFE

Pitseolak lived to watch rapid and extreme change take place in her Canadian Arctic homeland. Much of her life she lived in the traditional Inuit way, on the land. Although in later years she enjoyed the comfort of a warm house, Pitseolak also missed life in the camps, which she described as a hard life, but a good and happy one. In her art, she was able to capture some of the richness and vitality of traditional Inuit ways, before that way of life vanished forever.

Pitseolak once said about her drawings, "I am going to keep on doing them until they tell me to stop. If no one tells me to stop, I shall make them as long as I am well. If I can, I'll make them even after I am dead."

Pitseolak died in Cape Dorset, Northwest Territories at the age of seventy-nine.

Further suggested reading:

Eber, Dorothy, ed. *Pitseolak: Pictures Out of My Life*. Montreal: Design Collaborative Books and Oxford University Press, 1971.

TIME LINE

Note: Modern place names are used

1500s/1600s

1535   Jacques Cartier sails up the St. Lawrence River to Hochelaga

1608   Samuel de Champlain founds the colony of New France in Quebec

1670   King Charles II of England grants Rupert's Land to the Hudson's Bay Company

1696   Eunice Williams is born

1700s

1704   Eunice Williams and her family are kidnapped

1762   Marie-Henriette Lejeune (Ross) is born

1776   The American Revolution begins

1781   The American Revolution ends

1785   The Lejeune family settles on Cape Breton Island

1785   Eunice Williams dies

1791   Quebec is divided into Upper and Lower Canada

1792   Marie-Henriette Lejeune marries James Ross

1800s

1812   The War of 1812 - 1814 begins between Great Britain and the United States

1820   Emily Shaw (Beavan) is born

1835   Catherine O'Hare (Schubert) is born

1838   Frances Anne Beechey (Hopkins) is born

1838   Emily Shaw marries Dr. Frederick Beavan

1839   Sylvia Estes (Stark) is born

1841   Upper and Lower Canada are united as the Province of Canada

1845   Emily Shaw Beavan's *Sketches and Tales* is published in England

1851   Sylvia Estes (Stark) takes the "Overland Trek" to California

1855   Catherine O'Hare marries Augustus Schubert

1855   Sylvia Estes marries Louis Stark

1857   Adelaide Hunter (Hoodless) is born

1858   Frances Anne Beechey marries Edward Hopkins

1860 Marie-Henriette Lejeune Ross dies

1860 Sylvia Estes Stark and her family move to Saltspring Island

1861 The American Civil War begins

1861 Victoria Callihoo is born

1862 Catherine O'Hare Schubert and her family join the Overlanders of '62

1865 The American Civil War ends

1867 Confederation: The Dominion of Canada, made up of the provinces of Ontario, Quebec, New Brunswick and Nova Scotia, is formed

1869 Maude Abbott is born

1869 *Canoes in a Fog* is Frances Anne Hopkins' first painting to be exhibited at the Royal Academy, London, England

1870 Manitoba joins Confederation

1871 British Columbia joins Confederation

1873 Prince Edward Island joins Confederation

1873 Mary Riter (Hamilton) is born

1874 Victoria Callihoo goes on her first buffalo hunt

1876 Harriet Brooks (Pitcher) is born

1881 Catherine O'Hare Schubert settles in the Okanagan Valley

1883 Ontario Medical College for Women opens in Toronto, Ontario

1884 McGill University begins to accept women students in the arts

1887 Millie Gamble is born in Prince Edward Island

1889 Mary Riter marries Charles Hamilton

1890 Agnes Macphail is born

1890 Maude Abbott graduates from McGill with her B.A.

1891 Edna Jaques is born

1893 Charles Hamilton, husband of Mary Riter Hamilton, dies

1894 Margaret Duley is born

1894 Maude Abbott graduates from Bishop's Medical College, Montreal

1897 The Women's Institute is founded

1897 The Victorian Order of Nurses is founded by Lady Aberdeen

1897 Dr. Maude Abbott sets up her medical practice in Montreal

1898   Harriet Brooks graduates from McGill with an honours degree in mathematics and natural philosophy

1899   Harriet Brooks begins research on radioactivity

1900s

1901   Harriet Brooks receives her masters degree in physics from McGill

1904   Pitseolak is born

1904   Millie Gamble begins taking photographs

1905   Saskatchewan and Alberta join Confederation

1905   Three paintings by Mary Riter Hamilton are exhibited in the Salon of the Academy in France

1906   Harriet Brooks conducts research in France with Dr. Marie Curie

1907   Harriet Brooks marries Frank Pitcher

1910   Adelaide Hunter Hoodless dies

1914   World War I begins

1914   The Women's Patriotic Association is established in Newfoundland

1916   Women win the right to vote and hold political office in Manitoba, Saskatchewan and Alberta

1917   Women win the right to vote in British Columbia and Ontario

1917   Women are admitted into McGill Medical School

1918   World War I ends

1918   Catherine O'Hare Schubert dies

1918   Women win the right to vote and hold political office in Nova Scotia

1918   Women who have the right to vote in their own provincial elections have the right to vote in federal elections

1919   Frances Anne Hopkins dies

1919   Women win the right to run for office in federal elections

1919   Women win the right to vote in New Brunswick

1919   Mary Riter Hamilton returns to Europe to make battlefield paintings

1921   Agnes Macphail becomes the first woman member of Parliament

1921   Edna Jaques marries Ernest Jamieson

1922   Women win the right to vote and hold political office in Prince Edward Island

1922   Mary Riter Hamilton is awarded the purple ribbon of Les Palmes Académiques in France

1925	Women win the right to vote and hold political office in Newfoundland
1926	Monument erected in honour of Catherine O'Hare Schubert
1926	Mary Riter Hamilton donates 227 of her battlefield works to the National Archives of Canada
1929	Canadian women are, by law, declared to be "persons"
1933	Harriet Brooks Pitcher dies
1934	Commission Government is established in Newfoundland
1936	Margaret Duley's first novel, *The Eyes of the Gull*, is published
1939	World War II begins
1940	Women win the right to vote and hold political office in Quebec
1940	Dr. Maude Abbott dies
1943	Agnes Macphail elected to the Ontario Legislature
1944	Sylvia Estes Stark dies
1945	World War II ends
1949	Newfoundland joins Confederation
1954	Mary Riter Hamilton dies
1954	Agnes Macphail dies
1966	Victoria Callihoo dies
1968	Margaret Duly dies
1971	*Pitseolak: Pictures out of My Life* is published
1974	Pitseolak is elected a member of the Royal Academy of the Arts
1976	Edna Jaques is named "Woman of the Year" by the premier of Ontario
1977	Pitseolak receives the Order of Canada
1977	Edna Jaques' autobiography, *Uphill All the Way*, is published
1978	Edna Jaques dies
1983	Pitseolak dies
1986	Millie Gamble dies

Her Story II: Women From Canada's Past:
Select Bibliography

Ainley, Marianne Gosztonyi, ed. *Despite the Odds: Essays on Canadian Women and Science.* Montreal:Véhicule Press. 1990.

Backhouse, Constance. *Petticoats and Prejudice.* Toronto: The Osgoode Society, 1991.

Bataille, Gretchen M., ed. *Native American Women.* New York: Garland Publishing, 1993.

Beavan, Mrs. Francis. *Sketches and Tales Illustrative of Life in the backwoods of New Brunswick.* London: George Routledge, 1845. Reprinted. St. Stephen, New Brunswick: Print'n Press Publications Ltd., 1980.

Bennett, Jennifer. *Lilies of the Hearth.* Camden East, Ontario: Camden House Publishing, 1991.

Birch, Beverly. *Marie Curie: Radium Scientist.* London: Macdonald Educational Ltd, 1977.

Bramble, Linda. *Black Fugitive Slaves in Early Canada.* St. Catharines: Vanwell Publishing Limited, 1988.

Callihoo, Victoria. "Early life in Lac Ste. Anne and St. Albert in the Eighteen Seventies". *Alberta Historical Review* 1,no.3, (November 1953): 21-6.

Callihoo, Victoria. "Our Buffalo Hunts". *Alberta Historical Review* 8, no.1, (Winter 1960): 24-5.

Calloway, Colin G., compiler. *North Country Captives.* Hanover: University Press of New England, 1992.

Cardinal, Phyllis, and Dale Ripley. *The Métis.* Edmonton: Plain Publishing Inc., 1987.

Cavanaugh, Catherine A., and Randi R. Warne, eds. *Standing on New Ground:Women in Alberta.* Edmonton: University of Alberta Press, 1993.

Clark, Janet E., and Robert Stacey. *Frances Anne Hopkins 1838 - 1919: Canadian Scenery.* Thunder Bay: Thunder Bay Art Gallery, 1990.

Coe, Brian. *The Birth of Photography.* New York: Taplinger Publishing Company, 1977.

Creese, Gillian, and Veronica Strong-Boag, eds. *British Columbia Reconsidered.* Vancouver: Press Gang Publishers, 1992.

Dictionary of Canadian Biography

Duley, Margot I. *Where Once Our Mothers Stood We Stand :Women's Suffrage in Newfoundland 1890 - 1925.* Charlottetown: gynergy books, 1993.

Eber, Dorothy, ed. *Pitseolak: Pictures Out of My Life.* Montreal: Design Collaborative Books and Oxford University Press, 1971.

Eccles, W.J. *The Canadian Frontier.* Albuquerque: University of New Mexico Press, 1974.

Ehrenreich, Barbara, and Deirdre English. *For Her Own Good.* New York: Anchor Books Doubleday, 1978.

Feder, Alison. *Margaret Duley: Newfoundland Novelist, a Biographical and Critical Study.* St. John's: Harry Cuff Publications Limited, 1983.

Forbes, Malcolm. *Women Who Made A Difference.* New York: Simon & Schuster, 1990.

Gough, Barry. *Gold Rush!* Toronto: Grolier Limited, 1983.

Gould, Jan. *The Women of British Columbia.* Saanichton, British Columbia: Hancock House Publishers Ltd., 1975.

Greenhill, Ralph and Andrew Birrell. *Canadian Photography 1839 - 1920.* Toronto: Coach House Press, 1979.

Hacker, Carlotta. *The Indomitable Lady Doctors.* Toronto: Clarke, Irwin, 1974.

Harper, Russell J. "William Hind and the Overlanders". *The Beaver*, Winter 1971, 4 - 15.

Harper, Russell J. *Painting in Canada.* Toronto: University of Toronto Press, 1966.

Hill, Lawrence. *Trials and Triumphs: The Story of African-Canadians.* Toronto: Umbrella Press, 1993.

Innis, Mary Quayle, ed. *The Clear Spirit.* Toronto: University of Toronto Press, 1966.

Jaques, Edna. *Uphill All the Way.* Saskatoon: Western Producer Prairie Books, 1977.

Johnson, A. M. "Edward and Frances Hopkins of Montreal". *The Beaver,* Autumn 1971, 4 - 19.

Jones, Laura. *Rediscovery: Canadian Women Photographers 1841 - 1941.* London, Ontario: London Regional Art Gallery, 1983. (London Regional Art Gallery Catalogue May 13 - June 27, 1983)

Kahn, Charles and Maureen. *Canadians All 3: Portraits of Our People.* Toronto: Methuen, n.d.

Killian, Crawford. *Go Do Some Great Thing: The Black Pioneers of British Columbia.* Vancouver: Douglas & McIntyre, 1978.

Light, Beth, and Alison Prentice, eds. *Pioneer and Gentlewomen of British North America 1713 - 1867.* Toronto: New Hogtown Press, 1980.

Light, Beth, and Joy Parr, eds. *Canadian Women on the Move 1867-1920.* Toronto: New Hogtown Press and the Ontario Institute for Studies in Education, 1983.

Light, Beth, and Ruth Roach Pierson, eds. *No Easy Road: Women in Canada 1920's to 1960's.* Toronto: New Hogstown Press, 1990.

MacEwan, Grant. *. . . And Mighty Women Too.* Saskatoon: Western Producer Prairie Books, 1975.

MacEwan, Grant. *Métis Makers of History*. Saskatoon: Western Producer Prairie Books. 1981.

Mason, Jutta. *A History of Midwifery in Canada*. Report of the Task Force on the Implementation of Midwifery in Ontario. Toronto, 1987.

Metcalf, Vicky. *Catherine Schubert*. Toronto: Fitzhenry & Whiteside Limited, 1978.

Morton, Desmond. *New France and War*. Toronto: Grolier Limited, 1983.

Neering, Rosemary. *Gold Rush*. Toronto: Fitzhenry and Whiteside. 1974.

Newhall, Beaumont. *The History of Photography*. New York: Museum of Modern Art, 1978.

Norcross, E. Blanche. *Pioneers Every One*. Toronto: Burns & MacEachern Limited, 1979.

Nunn, Pamela Gerrish. *Victorian Women Artists*. London: The Women's Press Ltd., n.d.

Patterson, Palmer. *Inuit Peoples of Canada*. Toronto: Grolier Limited, 1988.

Prentice, Alison, Paula Bourre, Gail Cuthbert Brandt, Beth Light, Wendy Mitchinson, Naomi Black, eds. *Canadian Women: A History*. Toronto: Harcourt, Brace, Jovanovich, 1988.

Rayner-Canham, Marelene F., and Geoffrey W. Rayner-Canham. *Harriet Brooks:Pioneer Nuclear Scientist*. Montreal & Kingston: McGill-Queens University Press, 1992.

Reeves, John. "Women Artists of Cape Dorset". *City and Country Home* April 1985, 35 - 42.

Schlissel, Lillian, ed. *Women's Diaries of the Westward Journey*. NewYork: Schocken Books Inc., 1982.

Schreiber, June. *Alberta's Métis*. Edmonton: Reidmore Books, 1988.

Scott, Irene G. *The Trek of the Overlanders*. Toronto: Burns and MacEachern Limited, 1968.

Scott, Victoria, and Ernest Jones. *Sylvia Stark, a pioneer*. Seattle: Open Hand Publishing Inc., 1991.

Seaver, James E. *A Narrative in the Life of Mrs. Mary Jemison*. np: Syracuse University Press, 1990.

Stewart, Margaret and Doris French. *Ask No Quarter*. Toronto: Longmans, Green and Company, 1959.

Strasser, Susan. *Never Done: A History of American Housework*. New York: Pantheon Books, 1982.

Wilson, Keith. *The Fur Trade in Canada*. Toronto: Grolier Limited, 1983.

Wright, Ronald. *Stolen Continents*. Toronto: Penguin Books, 1993.

Ziner, Feenie. *The Pilgrims and the Plymouth Colony*. New York: American Heritage Publishing Co., Inc., 1961.

INDEX

PHOTO CREDITS - HER STORY II

EUNICE WILLIAMS (1696 - 1785)
1.1 ROM/ HD12702/ Iroquois Corn Husk Doll
1.2 Glenbow/ NA-1681-6 / Chippewa or Ojibwa woman and child, nd, "child in decorated headboard"
1.3 Glenbow/ NA-395 11/ "Siupako and Sikunnacio, Sarcee Indian girls" ca 1887
1.4 Prov. Arc Alta/ A3249/ "unidentified Indian women"
1.5 Prov. Arc Alta/ A18806 / 2 Cree women, Fort Walsh, nd
1.6 Glenbow/ NA-935-1 / Sioux wife of George Pembridge, NWMP, Fort Walsh c. 1878. Niece of Sitting Bull

MARIE-HENRIETTE LEJEUNE ROSS (1762 - 1860)
2.1 NAC/ C-004745/ Galicians at Immigration sheds, Quebec, nd
2.2 NAC/ 088632/ George E. Dragan Collection/ Glowaski family, Sask., nd
2.3 PA 114727/ Inuit woman and child
2.4 C 20815/ Assiniboine mother holding baby
2.5 NAC/ PA113084/ Gertrude H. Ross bathing Ian & Eugenia Ross, Montreal, 1898/John Wardrope Ross collection

EMILY SHAW BEAVAN (b. circa 1820)
3.1 National Gallery of Canada, Ottawa /*A Meeting of The School Trustees*/ Robert Harris
3.2 NAC/ C-018190/ Log City, N.B. June-Aug 1875 Photographer Alexander Henderson
3.3 Glenbow / NA-2925-18/ Gus Roland's log house, Content, Alta, c. 1908. Emigrants from England in 1900.
3.4 NAC/ C-007780/ A new Homestead east of Sugarloaf, NWT 1912. Photographer F. A. Fletcher
3.5 NCA/ PA-126654/ Unidentified woman with churn near Long Branch, Ont., 1893 Photograher W. Braybrooke Bayley

CATHERINE O'HARE SCHUBERT (1835 - 1918)
4.1 NAC/ C9583/ *Overlanders setting out from Fort Gary* by W.G.R. Hind
4.2 NAC/ C13969/ *Duck Hunting on the prairies* by W.G.R.Hind
4.3 Provincial Archives of Alberta/ B670/ Homesteaders Pembina area C.1905
4.4 Glenbow/ NA-1328-2832 / Honeymoon couple on sled, Edson-Grand Prairie trail, Alta. 1914. 'En route to homestead'
4.5 Prov. Arc Alta/ A. 11,455 / Homesteaders waiting for the boat, Peace River Crossing c 1910

FRANCES ANNE HOPKINS (1838 - 1918)
5.1 McCord Museum of Canadian History, Notman Photographic Archives/ 8274-I/ Frances Anne Hopkins 1863
5.2 Glenbow, Calgary, Alberta 55.8.1 / *Canoes in a Fog*/ Frances Anne Hopkins
5.3 NAC/ C2771/ *Canoe Manned by Voyageurs Passing A Waterfall*/ Frances Anne Hopkins
5.4 NAC/ C-002773/ *Voyageurs at Dawn*, 1871 Frances Anne Hopkins
5.5 NAC/ C2772/ *Canoe Party Around Campfire*/ Frances Anne Hopkins
5.6 NAC/ C134842/ X-ray of *Canoe Party Around Campfire*/ Frances Anne Hopkins
5.7 NAC/ C2774/ *Shooting the Rapids*/ Frances Anne Hopkins

SYLVIA ESTES STARK (1839 - 1944)
6.1 NA-263-1/ John Ware and family, black rancher. c. 1896 "Mrs. Ware, Robert, Nettie and John Ware"

6.2 Province of British Columbia Archives / 2209 A-1068 / Charles and Nancy Alexander

6.3 City of Vancouver Archives/Port.P.67, N.68#3/ "Mrs. Josephine Sullivan," whom Rev. Tate says was the "first Methodist in Vancouver"

6.4 Province of British Columbia Archives/ 25242 A-9481/ Mary Lowe Barnsworth

ADELAIDE HUNTER HOODLESS (1857 - 1910)

7.1 NAC/ C30937/ 'The one room home'/ Lewis W. Hine

7.2 NAC/ PA131939/ Margaret Hyde ironing clothes, Ottawa 1892, photo by James or May Ballantyne

7.3 NAC/ PA 800211/ Beales, Arthur / Mrs. Arthur Beales in the kitchen of the Beales home. Toronto c. 1903-1913

7.4 Saskatchewan Archives Board/ R-A4809/ Hulda Swedberg, daughter of a Swedish-American immigrant from Minnesota, in her kitchen, Marchwell district(sic), 1906

7.5 Glenbow/ NC-43-12/ Pioneer woman churning butter, Mrs. H.B. Biggs, Springfield Ranch, Beynon, Alta, ca. 1908.

VICTORIA BELCOURT CALLIHOO (1861 - 1966)

8.1 Provincial Archives of Manitoba/ N16374/ Breland (Pascal) Family Collection 15, n.d. - unidentified family

8.2 NAC/ C 1732/ Laetitia Bird, "Cree Halfbreed" 1858

8.3 Saskatchewan Archives Board/ R-B1627/ Three Indian Women, ca. 1905

8.4 Glenbow/ NA-4581-3 / Blackfoot Indian girl with cat, Fort Macleod, Alt. c 1880

8.5 Glenbow/ NC-7-852 / Blood Indian woman, nd

DR. MAUDE ABBOTT (1869 - 1940)

9.1 NAC/ C-9479/ Maude Elizabeth Seymour Abbott

9.2 LH2867/ Marcel Photo/ Saskatoon Public Library-Local History Room/ Fanny Sperry-Steele, World Champion Lady Bucking-Horse Rider, Winnipeg Stampede 1913

9.3 Glenbow Archives/ NA-1758-15 / Grand Trunk Pacific railway construction near Viking, Alta, c. 1907

9.4 NAC/ C-018864/ Women operating cartidge case presses (Canadian Allis-Chalmers, Limited) 1914-1918

9.5 NA-2083-6/ Sawing wood on Andrew Parkkari's farm near Alderson, Alberta

9.6 NAC/C 6794/ Class in Surgery, 1890, with the Dean, Hon. Senator Sullivan, Kingston Women's Medical College

9.7 NAC/ PA-123087/ Field, G.H./ Resident staff, Toronto General Hospital, Feb. 1895. G.H. Field is at right.

MARY RITER HAMILTON (1873 - 1954)

10.1 Courtesy of the E.P. Taylor Reference Library and Archives, Art Gallery of Ontario/ (neg. # PH-602-1)/ Portrait of Mrs. Mary Riter Hamilton (as illustrated in Canadian Magazine, Oct. 1912)

10.2 NAC/ C-132012/ *Market Among the Ruins of Ypres*, 1920, Mary Riter Hamilton

10.3 NAC/ C-104742/ *Sanctuary Wood*, Flanders, 1920, Mary Riter Hamilton

10.4 NAC/ 104640/ *Canadian Monument, Passchendaele Ridge*, ca. 1920, Mary Riter Hamilton

10.5 NAC/C142436/ *Ravages of War*, ca. 1920, Mary Riter Hamilton

HARRIET BROOKS PITCHER (1876 - 1933)

11.1 McCord Museum of Canadian History, Notman Photographic Archives 123,880 - B II/ Harriet Brooks, graduation photograph, 1898

11.2 McCord Museum of Canadian History, Notman Photographic Archives 92010 - B II/ Carrie Derrick, 1890

11.3 McCord Museum of Canadian History, Notman Photographic Archives MP016/89 (2)/ Maude E. Abbott and friends in Scotland c. 1895

11.4 University of Toronto Archives/ A73-0026/318 (11a)/ Graduation photograph of Maud L. Menten

MILLIE GAMBLE (1887 - 1986)

12.1 Women in front of J.F. Lord's store, North Tryon, PAPEI 2667/123

12.2 Ladies of the Tryon Baptist Church, PAPEI 2667/136

12.3 The Ives family fishing, PAPEI 2667/ (no other # on photo)

12.4 Women berry picking, PAPEI 2667/147

12.5 Adelaide and Hope Ives playing with toys, PAPEI 2667/132

12.6 Hope and Adelaide Ives sitting on sacks in a field, PAPEI 2667/140

12.7 Women and children working in the field, PAPEI 2667/131

AGNES MACPHAIL (1890 - 1954)

13.1 NAC/ C 6908/ Agnes Macphail 1921/ Kelsey Studio

13.2 Public Archives of Alberta/ H530/ Nisbet School, Sept 24, 1908

13.3 NAC/ PA 88504/ Ukrainian family in wheatfield

13.4 Glenbow/ NC-43-13/ "Woman cutting oats with team and mower, Beynon, Alberta," c. 1909

13.5 NAC/ 6C16926/ Harvesting potato crop/ Manitoba/Canadian National Railways

EDNA JAQUES (1891-1978)

14.1 University of Guelph Library/ David L. Gibson Collection/ women washing clothes on Keewaydin Island, Ontario

14.2 Western Canada Pictorial Index, University of Winnipeg/ 424-14245/ Woman washing clothes in a wringer washing machine. From Brandon Museum collection.

14.3 NA-2041-1/ Laundry day on Wyman's farm, near Bon Accord, Alta. c.late teens. Mrs. John Payzant washing clothes outside

14.4 Glenbow/ NA-1789-3/ Wash day at sod shack, Delia area. c. early teens. Florence Lewis and Mrs. John Larson hanging clothes

14.5 Glenbow/ NA-1367-7/ Stooking in Milo district c. 1923 (photo by Jessie Burk Umscheid) Mrs. Ernest Burke, centre

14.6 Glenbow/ NA-1367-74/ Jessie Burk's mother and sister digging potatoes, c.1916/ photo by Jessie Burk Umscheid

MARGARET DULEY (1894- 1968)

15.1 PA Nfld & Lab/ NA 2060 / Picnic at Forest Pond

15.2 PA Nfld & Lab/ B5-173/ Women's Patriotic Association - Workers WWI

15.3 PA Nfld & Lab/ NA 3730/ Ross' Farm, Pleasantville

15.4 PA Nfld & Lab/ NA 2972/ Quidi Vidi Village

15.5 PA Nfld & Lab./ VA14-192/ Standing woman

PITSEOLAK (1904 - 1983)

16.1 Canada Post Corporation/ Pitseolak $.43 stamp

16.2 NAC/ C 23933/ Inuit girl from Mackenzie River area

16.3 NAC/ PA 53606/ women in beaded Atigit, 1903-4

16.4 NAC/ PA 53548/ Portrait of Shoofly Comer, A.P. Low Expedition 1903-4

16.5 Canada Post Corporation/ Pitseolak $.14 stamp

ABOUT THE AUTHOR

SUSAN E. MERRITT received a B.A. in English and a law degree from the University of Western Ontario. While at Western, she won an English scholarship and an award for English composition and speech. Susan has researched and spoken widely upon the topic of women in history and has appeared on numerous CBC radio and television programs. Her first book, Her Story : Women from Canada's Past, became a best-seller and was named a Canadian Library Association Notable for 1993. Susan lives in Ridgeway, Ontario, with her husband and two children.